Kush, the Jewel of Nubia—

☥

Reconnecting the Root System of African Civilization

KUSH, THE JEWEL OF NUBIA—

RECONNECTING THE ROOT SYSTEM OF AFRICAN CIVILIZATION

MIRIAM MAÁT-KA-RE MONGES

Africa World Press, Inc.

P.O. Box 1892
Trenton, NJ 08607

P.O. Box 48
Asmara, ERITREA

Africa World Press, Inc.

P.O. Box 1892
Trenton, NJ 08607

P.O. Box 48
Asmara, ERITREA

Copyright © 1997 Miriam Ma'at-Ka-Re Monges

First Printing 1997

All rights reserved. No part of this publication may be reproduced, stored in a retrieval system or transmitted in any form or by any means electronic, mechanical, photocopying, recording or otherwise without the prior written permission of the publisher.

Cover design: Linda Nickens & Aaron J. Wilson

Library of Congress Cataloging-in-Publication Data

Monges, Miriam Ma'at-Ka-Re.
   Kush, the jewel of Nubia : reconnecting the root system of African civilization / Miriam Ma'at-Ka-Re Monges.
      p. cm.
   Includes bibliographical references and index.
   ISBN 0-86543-528-6 (cloth : alk. paper). -- ISBN 0-86543-529-4 (pbk.: alk. paper)
   1. Nubia--Civilization. 2. Africa--Civilization. I. Title.
DT159.6.N83M66   1996
939'.78-dc20   96-43315
                                                                                       CIP

DEDICATION

This book is dedicated to Cheikh Anta Diop--a valiant and committed scholar who with undaunted courage struggled for the liberation of African people. In the tradition of *Maát*, he brought order to the chaos of the Eurocentric perspective of African historiography.

May this book add to his legacy.

La luta continua.

ACKNOWLEDGMENTS

Before the great Kushite king Piankhi entered into battle to save ancient Kemet from the invaders, he instructed his army not to attack before they asked the Divine creator, Amun, for counsel. He advised his army that success in battle was not to be attributed to the power of bows, but to the power of the spirit. He and his army participated in rituals honoring the Divine Creator and strengthening their kas before they entered into battle. In the tradition of Piankhi, I would like to thank those who have helped me to strengthen my ka by contributing their support to this book.

First, I would like to thank Professors Thad Mathis, Abu Abarry, Nigun Okur, Terry Kershaw, C.T. Keto, Sonja Peterson-Lewis, Kariamu Welsh Asante; Wade Nobles, a mentor and wise advisor, who gave me excellent counsel and support; and Theophile Obenga, a paragon of a dedicated scholar, for his guidance, support, and lessons in precise scholarship. A special thanks to the spirit of Professor Vivian Gordon who was an inspiration to me. She gave me, a financially challenged graduate student, her bibliography on Kemet and encouraged my search for knowledge. Above all, I am indebted to Professor Molefi Asante, who conceived and developed the theory of Afrocentricity, without which this book would be impossible. Professor Molefi Asante's advocacy, guidance, and reassurance were critical to the ultimate realization of this book.

I would be remiss if I did not thank my friends, Marline Paramour, Ron O'Neal, John Groce, Richard Cooper, A. Delores Davis, Jarma Frisby, Michael Clemmons, Viola Malone, Vera Nobles, Steve Reddick, Charles Peoples, Mark at the University of Pennsylvania Museum library, Catherine Godbolte, Doreen Loury, Simon Kyoto, Norma Folk, Gerri Ambush, Gail Hoffman, Mike Griffin, Rafiki Webster, Sharon Andrade, and my Nzingha sisters, Frankye Adams, Dena Green Brown and Odunfunda for believing in me. A very special thanks is given to the elder Nzingha sister, Helen Jones, who edited my work with alertness and accuracy; and my friend, Toni Oliver, who made order out of chaos, by preparing an index for me.

I am indebted to the many people at CSU, Chico who supported this book, in particular, Provost Scott McNall, Dean Jim Jacob, Associate Dean Byron Jackson, Chair Clark Davis, and Professors Hassan Sisay, Jan O'Donnell, Carol Burr, Robert Jackson, Robert Bakke, and the support staff Billie Kanter, Jolee Liptrap and Candy Priano. I want to give thanks to Professor Eugenie Rovai and Lora Richards who were instrumental in developing the map. Additionally, a special thanks to Jana Lawton and her staff, who expertly pulled the book together and put the finishing touches on it.

Lastly, it is impossible to measure the support that my family has provided me. My cup runneth over. I am indebted to my sisters, Renee Allbritton and Lois Loftin; my brothers, my aunts and uncles, particularly, Eleanor Finney and Paul Harris, and numerous cousins; my former in laws who are now part of my extended family, the Mongeses, who have always supported my efforts; my mother, who is now among the ancestors who give me strength and guidance and who instilled love of learning in me; my father, Walter Holland, who has always been an independent thinker and provided a reservoir of relief. My most heartfelt gratitude is reserved for my beloved children, Taína Afaph and Caliph Caribe, who gave me the space, time, and love that I needed to complete this work. I am proud of their achievements as I hope they are proud of mine. Above all to my ancestors, who have left a well of strength and perseverance from whose waters I frequently drink. May the ancestors be satisfied.

CONTENTS

ACKNOWLEDGMENTS vi

MAP xii

CHAPTER ONE
ANCESTRAL BEGINNINGS 1

    The Meroitic Period 5
    Where Was Nubia? 6

CHAPTER TWO
CLEARING A MUDDLED PERSPECTIVE 19

    "African Civilization
    Not African" Literature 19
    "Meroe Not An African Culture" Literature 40
    Intellectual Heritage of Eurocentrism 44
    Homage to the Elders 52
    Summary 60

CHAPTER THREE
EMANCIPATING THE STUDY OF
AFRICAN CULTURE AND HISTORY 63

CHAPTER FOUR
AFRICAN CULTURAL COMMONALITIES 69

Petrie's *Egypt in Africa* 69
Linguistic Connections 72
Parallels in African Religions 73
Seligman's "Egyptian Influence in Negro Africa" 76
Jeffreys' *Diffusion of Cowries And*
Egyptian Culture in Africa 78
H. Frankfort on "Modern Survivors From Punt" 80
Diffusionist Theory 81

CHAPTER FIVE
DIVINE KINGSHIP 89

Nubian Origins of Divine Kingship 89
Arguments Against Nubian Origins of Divine Kingship . 98
Constituents of Divine Kingship 102
The Ritual Killing of the King 106
Kush and Divine Kingship 111
Piankhi 114
Stela of King Taharqa 120
Summary 121

CHAPTER SIX
MATRIARCHY: EXAMINING THE EXALTED
POSITION OF WOMEN IN KEMET AND KUSH 125

Diop's Two Cradle Theory 126
Intellectual Foundations of Matriarchy 130
Mothers of Kush 134
God's Wife of Amun 137
The Kandakes 140
Kandake Amanishakheto 147
Kandake Amanitere 149
Queen Nawidemak 150
Summary 152

CHAPTER SEVEN
TOTEMISM AND COSMOGONY: SURVEYING THE SACRED 155

Arguments in Support of the Existence of
Totemism 156
Totemism as a Religion, or the Relation
Between a Man and His Totem 156
Social Aspect of Totemism, or the Relation of
the People of a Totem to Each Other and to
People of Other Totems 158
The Origin of Totemism 159
Totemism as a Religious System 161
Totemism in Ancient Egypt 162
Arguments Against Totemism 165
Cosmogony 171
Totemism in Kush 175
Amun 175
The Color Blue 176
Amun as a Ram-God 178

CHAPTER EIGHT
NOT THE END: SUMMARY, RECOMMENDATIONS, AND CONCLUSION 185

GLOSSARY 189

SELECTED BIBLIOGRAPHY 193

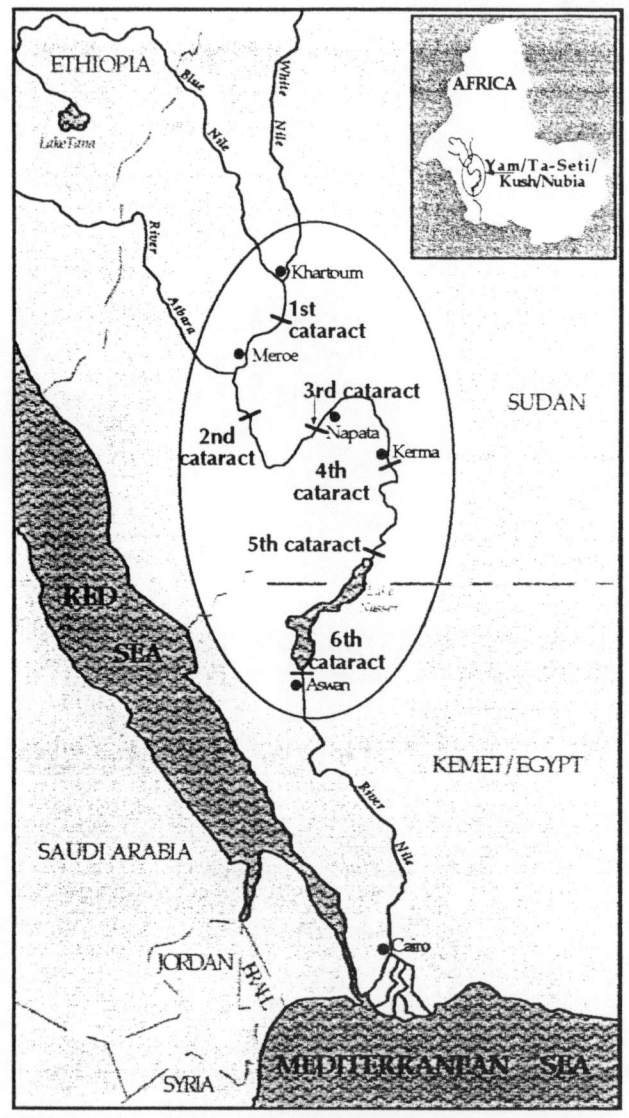

The World As Seen By The Ancient Africans

This is a map of the ancient Nile Valley, which contains the area known in various times in history as: Yam/Ta-Seti/Kush/Nubia. I have changed the orientation so that we can see the world from an Afrocentric perspective.

CHAPTER ONE

ANCESTRAL BEGINNINGS

> I've known rivers:
> I've known rivers ancient as the world and
> older than the flow of human blood in human veins.
> My soul has grown deep like the rivers...
> I looked upon the Nile and raised the pyramids above it...
> --Langston Hughes,
> *The Negro Speaks of Rivers*[1]

In 1992, I stood on the balcony of a hotel in Cairo, overlooking the Nile, and thanked the ancestors for bringing me to a land once called Kemet, the Land of the Blacks. It had been a longtime goal of mine to come to Egypt. Here I was laying my eyes on the Nile, the river whose rising and falling gave the ancient people nourishment not only for the body, but also for the soul. The ancient Africans saw in the Nile a paradigm of the cycle of life, death, and regeneration. Without the Nile, there would have been no Kemet, no Nubia, no sphinx, no pyramids, no Valley of the Kings. Here I was laying eyes on the same river and scenes as once had Queen Hatshepsut. I could only humble myself and thank the ancestors.

Later, while sailing up the river, we encountered many beautiful coal-black people, adeptly sailing their ships on the Nile and selling their goods in the market. They called themselves Nubians and spoke a language called Nubian. They sometimes rode camels, with style and a pose that reminded me of what the Black people in the United States call attitude. They were splendid. They greeted the tour group of African-Americans as brothers and sisters and marveled at the similarity of our skin color. We had come to the part of present-day Egypt that was once ruled by these Black people called Nubians. Majestically arrayed, the area—now called Aswan and Abu Simbel—is filled with gigantic stone edifices, such as Ramses' tombs. These gargantuan tombs are breathtaking from the outside; inside however are equally awesome scenes of Nefertari-Meri-En-Mut, Ramses' beloved queen of Nubian ancestry, flanked by the goddesses Hathor and Auset, which inspired me to learn more about Nubians.

I learned that in Nubia lay many of the components of the ancestral beginnings of dynastic Egypt. I learned that a kingdom called Meroe (Asante 1990) was located in Nubia; that Meroe was in a Nubian kingdom called Kush, and Meroe was preceded by a kingdom called Napata. Out of Kush came Taharqa and Piankhi, two kings who formed part of the high point of ancient Egyptian dynastic history, the 25th Dynasty. This civilization is vitally important to the reconstruction of African history.

Nubia was located south of ancient Egypt, firmly in Africa. Thus one would think it hard to dissociate Nubia from African culture. Yet I learned that it *has* been so dissociated. In Western historiography, scholars instinctively disconnect the great civilizations of Africa from African people themselves. There are numerous examples of this, from the building of the pyramids of Egypt to the great walls of Zimbabwe. Western scholars usually attribute the achievements of these great civilizations to people outside of Africa. In this, they continue to obey the Hegelian doctrine which says that Africa is on the periphery of world history. This is the reason why Kemet (ancient

Egypt) is connected to the Near East or the Orient and disconnected from the African continent.

In the case of Nubia, one might reasonably assume that Western scholars would attribute this culture to African people. However, this is not the case even though ancient Greek historians—contemporaries of the Nubians—considered Nubia a land inhabited by black people. They called it Ethiopia. For these scholars, Ethiopia not only preceded ancient Egypt in the course of civilization, but actually donated its own intellectual and material infrastructure to its junior. Thus, it is important to look at this problem more closely because of the cloud obscuring the view of historical thought.

Only an Afrocentric approach will shine light on this murky subject, which is why this book has been written: to develop a methodology that will enable us to study the Nubian past from an African-centered point of view.

Since Cheikh Anta Diop's work, no African researcher has published a comprehensive analysis connecting Nubia with the African cultural universe. The writing of history about Nubia needs to be liberated and put back into the proper hands—i.e., *African* ones.

Nubia is important to African history. In Nubia, were born the components of divine kingship. Nubia also nurtured the legacy of Kemetic ancestors and revived the greatness of Kemet during the 25th Dynasty. Nubia supported Kemet by virtue of its position as a trading center between Kemet and other parts of Africa, and Africa's gold. Nubia not only guided Kemet during times of political turmoil but also taught Kemet lessons in revitalization. Nubia was indeed the "Mother of Kemet."

The Kingdom of Kush is the name given to a period of Nubian history during which there were two successive capitals, Napata and Meroe.

It is generally agreed that Kush extended from ca. 900 to ca. 350 B.C.E. The exact location of the administrative center of Napata is unknown (Adams 1977; Dixon 1964), but it was associated with the area surrounding the sacred mountain of Jebel Barkal, named by the ancients the "Holy Mountain" (*Dw w'b*). Excavations of the Oxford Expedition team under F. L. Griffith have unearthed masses of potsherds and other debris which provides evidence that suggests it may have been "at or near the modern district headquarters of Merowe, four miles downstream from Gebel Barkal on the east bank of the river" (Dixon 1964, 123). The location of the city near the sacred mountain must have been very significant because royal personages were still being buried there even after the capital was moved.

Because there are no written records concerning the origins of Napata, most theories of its origins have been derived from information gathered from excavations of the tombs found in the area. The earliest known monuments are thirty-six royal tombs in the cemetery of El Kurru. Reisner, the first (and still most quoted) authority on Kush, hypothesized that the rulers were from Libya and that their assumption of rule of Egypt, during the 25th Dynasty, was due to their kinship to the Libyan Pharaohs of the 22nd Dynasty (Reisner [2], 46-8). Most scholars now believe, however, that Reisner's hypothesis of Libyan origins for Kushite kings is untenable (Adams 1977; Dixon 1964) and it is generally agreed that the Kushite Kingdom was ruled by indigenous people. Although the chronology of this period is still undefined, it is now believed by some scholars that possibly as early as by 705 B.C.E. (Depuydt 1993, 269-274), Shabaka, a Kushite king, was powerful enough to save Kemet from foreign invaders. This launched the 25th Dynasty of Kemet. It was a union of Kemet and Kush and one of the most beloved and respected dynasties remembered by the Kemetic people.

The Napata phase of Kush has been divided into two periods. Dixon (1964), an archeologist, describes the periods as follows:

> ...the first [period], during which the Kushite monarchs...ruled an empire extending from the shores of the Mediterranean to at least as far south as the northern Gezira, lasted until 654 B.C., when the seat of

government was transferred from Napata further south to Meroe, which retained this status until the collapse of the kingdom in the fourth century of our era. (123)

The Meroitic Period

The Meroitic period is generally agreed to extend from the sixth century B.C.E. to the beginning of the fourth century C.E. (Dunham 1947, 10). The origin of the city of Meroe is also unknown. It is known that by 538 B.C.E., royalty were being buried at Napata, but ruling from Meroe. The first mention of Meroe in the annals of written history occurred when it was at the height of its power. Incorrectly called an island, it was a center of trade and one of several settlements located between the second and first cataracts of the Butanna Steepe, a triangular area formed by the confluence of the Atbara and Nile rivers. One archeologist, who has written extensively on Nubia, postulates that "Meroe...became the lifeline connecting the northern and southern districts of Kush...[and] Egypt as well. Beyond Meroe, a number of trade routes extended far into the interior of Africa" (Adams 1977, 303).

It is surmised that some event of political significance precipitated the transfer of the capital of Kush from Napata to Meroe. It may have been the result of the increase of trade routes to Meroe or it might have been because the Kushite rulers wanted to move away from the powerful priests at Amun temple at Jebel Barkal (Olsen & Wegner 1992, 13). This transfer marked the beginning of a cultural, economic, and artistic "Imhotepean" period[2] in the history of Kush, that is to say, there was a rebirth of artistic and political excellence. By the time of Ptolemaic (Greek) rule in Kemet, "it [Kush] was receiving taxes paid in kind or personal service and was presumably thought of as an effective force that protected important trade routes, grazing lands, and farms from desert marauders" (Drake 1987, 279).

In more recent times, Meroe was remembered because the Alexandrian scholar Eratosthenes, who in his calculation of the earth's diameter and distinction of seven latitudes, or climates, also used the geographical latitude of Meroe, which he established as 16° 51' north latitude. For cartographers, the "climate of Meroe" continued to be a distinct concept up until modern times (Priese 1992, 8).

Where Was Nubia?

There is considerable confusion concerning the location of Nubia. It no longer exists as a sovereign political entity. Moreover, during various times in history, different names have been applied to Nubia. As a consequence, there is considerable confusion over the matter of the location of Nubia. The following section seeks to elucidate some of the issues.

Jacob Carruthers, a professor of Inner City Studies and political science at Northeastern Illinois University and the director of the Kemetic Institute in Chicago, is also one of the founders of the Association for the Study of Classical African Civilization (ASCAC). Carruthers posits that "orientation" is fundamental to framing the context of the African world view:

> *Orient* [emphasis original]...refers to the East, particularly Asia. It conveys the idea of alignment or establishment of one's bearing...Thus, orientation connotes the setting right of something because East is on the right when one is facing North...*North, in a spatial sense, is associated with **up** because Europeans who originate in the North made the map*...South derives from... Sol, meaning sun. Occident, which refers to the *West,* derives from the concept of the setting sun [emphasis added] (Carruthers [1984] 1992, 19)

Clearly, the words that are commonly used to define orientation are rooted in the Eurocentric paradigm.

In order to locate time-and-space issues in the Nile Valley, within the Afrocentric perspective, one must first know from what perspective one is viewing the land. Keto (1989), in philosophical agreement with Carruthers, illuminates another dimension of the problem. He writes that "the most interesting contemporary display of the dominance of Europe-centered perspective is to be found in the continued preference of Mercator projection maps...*no maps are made with the southern hemisphere at the top although the earth as a sphere floating in space can be depicted accurately either way*" [emphasis added] (10).

The people of the Nile Valley, who were living on their own terms, had no orientation problems. Carruthers declares that:

> [T]he most ancient well-known civilization equated South with up and North with down. Thus, Asia is to the left of Egypt, not above it and what is now called the Sudan (the old Ethiopia) is above Egypt. Indeed, the major words for up and south are interchangeable...It is now time for us to stand on our feet as men and women and see the world rightly constructed. (20)

It is the aim of this book to seek to "see the world rightly constructed" by placing the cataracts of the Nile in the proper "orientation." This orientation will be the reverse of the orientation of Eurocentric scholars. The so-called "Sixth" Cataract, located in the heart of Africa, near the Butanna Steepe, is actually the First Cataract. The "Fifth" will be placed as the Second; the "Fourth" will be the Third; the "Third" will be the Fourth; the "Second" will be the Fifth; and lastly, the "First" will be the Sixth. In this manner, we will attempt to see the world as the ancient Africans saw it. In quotations by scholars, however, the orientations used by the authors will be given verbatim. This "southern" orientation of the ancient Africans is directly related to the flow of the Nile. Kemetologist Tony Browder, informs us that:

> The Nile Valley River system is the world's longest waterway (4,160)...An interesting fact about the Nile is that it...flow[s] south to north. The migratory pattern of the people who navigated the Nile, from "up south" to "down north," was to later play a major role in the development of civilization in ancient Egypt. (46)

The issue of the cultural origins of ancient Egypt will be examined more fully below, in the chapter concerning divine kingship. The point at present is that the Africans of the Nile Valley looked "up south" and "down north."

The language of the ancient Egyptians supports the "southern orientation" of the Kemites. The etymology of the word for *king*, in the hieroglyphics, is *nswt*. This word derives from *swt*, which is the word for the sedge plant, the plant of Upper Egypt. *Biti,* the word for Lower Egypt was never used to mean simply king (Diop [1981] 1991, 108).

The word for "west" in the mdu neter was *imnt*, a variation was *wnmi*, meaning "right" hand, side, etc. The word for east was *i3bt*, a variation was *i3bi* meaning "left-hand" (Gardiner [1927] 1992, 502).

Archeologist William Y. Adams (1977) in his section on geography of Nubia, seeks to shed some light on the placement of Nubia:

> The land known as Nubia lies today partly in Egypt and partly in the Republic of the Sudan, but comprises only a small part of either country. (20)

Therefore, states Adams (1977), what *was* ancient Nubia would now be located in *two* modern countries, Egypt and the Sudan.

> *The northern limit of Nubia is, and has always been, as sharply defined as the First Cataract [Sixth Cataract] itself.* The eastern

> and western limits are equally clearly marked...*It is only the southern, or upper, limit of Nubia which is difficult to define...* For precisely the historical reasons already noted, *there is no general agreement as to the boundaries of Nubia either in modern or in ancient times.* [emphasis added] (20)

Scholars have never been in complete agreement on the boundaries of Nubia. This is not to say that the Africans did not know where the boundaries lay; however, no one in modern times has determined them to the satisfaction of all. Scholars quibble the most about how far into Africa the boundaries of Nubia extended. S. Adams [1981] extends those "northern" boundaries into modern-day Ethiopia:

> We could define historical Nubia as that part of the Nile basin lying between *the west-north-west frontier of present-day Ethiopia and Egypt.* This includes the Nile valley itself, parts of the White Nile and Blue Nile, and all their tributaries above 12° north, such as Atbara, the Rahad and the Dindor. [emphasis added] (230)

I submit that the southern boundary is related to the issue of Nubia's relationship to the rest of Africa. For the present purposes, the northern geographical points outlined in the following passage from Olson & Wegner's *Ancient Nubia: Egypt's Rival in Africa* (1992) will be used. However, the orientation will be changed, as follows:

> The cataracts serve as markers of Nubia's borders. *The First Cataract [Afr: Sixth Cataract], just to the south of Aswan, marks the northern [southern] boundary of Nubia.* The [northern] border, though it has fluctuated over time, lies near the Sixth Cataract [African: First Cataract]...Lower Nubia includes the area between the First and

Second Cataracts. [African: Sixth and Fifth Cataracts] [emphasis added] (4) [see map]

One of the earliest names for Nubia was *Ta-Seti*, "the Land of the Bow." Based on evidence unearthed in Qustal, a city in Lower Nubia, it would appear that this may have been the name for Lower Nubia (Williams 1980, 19). The skill of these warriors with their bows remained legendary throughout the history of the ancient Nile Valley and there are those who hold that it was the name for all of Nubia (Emery 1965). Emery (1965) postulates that the ancient people of Ta-Seti distinguished the area between the First and Second [Afr: Sixth and Fifth Cataracts] as Wawat and south of the Second Cataract [Afr: Fifth Cataract] as Kush (16). We do know that the toponymies, *Ta-Seti* and *Wawat*, were used in ancient texts; however the location of these sites is all speculation.

One of the names for Lower Nubia used in the Kemetic text was *Yam*; its exact location is also not known. Adams (1977) states that "The name of Yam is never heard of after the Old Kingdom...it may or may not have lain to the south of the Second [Afr: Fifth] Cataract" (186). Yam was considered an affluent land by the ancient Egyptians.

The Pharaoh Mernere dispatched his official Harkhuf to Yam on four major expeditions for purposes of trade and to obtain soldiers (W.Y. Adams 1977, 186; Breasted 1912, 151; Emery 1965, 131). Harkhuf was one of Kemet's most esteemed ambassadors. He was a prominent member of the royal team. He served first under Mernere and, upon this Pharaoh's death, he served under Pepi II. His titles included "Count, sole companion, ritual priest... caravan-conductor, privy councilor of all affairs of the South, favorite of his lord" (Breasted 1906, I:No.332). His role as a priest was important to him. In his description of himself he informs the reader that "I am an excellent, equipped spirit, a ritual priest, whose mouth knows" (I, No.329). There was no separation of church and state in Kemet—or the rest of Africa—and he proudly combined both roles.

On Harkhuf's first journey to Yam, he "brought all (kinds of) gifts from it" (I, No.333). On his second voyage, it "being an affair of eight months. When I descended I brought gifts from this country in very great quantity" (54). On Harkhuf's third journey, he involved himself in the internal politics of the area. He encountered

> the chief of Yam going to the land of Temeh to smite Temeh...I went forth after him to the land of Temeh, and I pacified him.... Now when I had pacified that chief of Yam ...I found the chief of Irthet, Sethu and Wawat...I descended with three hundred asses laden with incense, ebony, heknu, grain, (panthers), ivory, (throw sticks), and every good product. Now when the chief of Irthet, Sethu, and Wawat saw how strong and numerous was the troop of Yam...(then) this (chief) brought and gave me bulls and small cattle, and conducted me to the roads of the highland of Irthet, because I was more excellent, vigilant...than any... caravan-conductor, who had been sent to Yam before. (Breasted 1912, I:No.335-6)

This text provides evidence of trade relationships among the African peoples of Kemet and Nubia. Breasted and others defined the Nubians as chiefs and the Kemites, whom they have disconnected from Africa, as kings. This distinction does not come from anything internal to the text. It is the expression of an Eurocentric paradigm that consistently deflates the position of African people. Yam was a rich land, judging from the amount and quality of the trade items. Harkhuf, who was an adventurer and a noble diplomat, brought back the most prized item on his next voyage.

Harkhuf's fourth expedition to Yam was for Pepi II. In the only complete royal letter from the Old Kingdom, Harkhuf wrote to the king to inform him that he was bringing him "a dancing dwarf of the god from the land of the spirits, like the dwarf which the treasurer Burded brought from Punt in the time of Isesi" (Breasted 1906, I, No.352). The king was extremely delighted. The king believed that this small person was the embodiment of powerful spiritual forces. Clearly, Pepi II placed high value on him:

> Thou shalt bring this dwarf with thee, which thou bringest living, prosperous and healthy from the land of the spirits, for the dances of the god, to rejoice and gladden the heart of the king. When he goes down with thee into the vessel, appoint excellent people, who shall be beside him on each side of the vessel; take care lest he fall into the water. When [he] sleeps at night appoint excellent people, who shall sleep beside him in his tent, inspect him ten times a night. My majesty desires to see this dwarf more than the gifts of Sinai and of Punt. (I,No.353)

We cannot be sure of the full significance of small people from Central Africa. However, from this passage we can glean some insight. The little person was a member of the so-called pygmies.[3] They lived in Central Africa. About them anthropologist George Peter Murdock (1959) writes:

> Under the name Sangoan archaeologists group a series of closely related prehistoric cultures found in central Africa...Their bearers were hunting and gathering people who centered in the equatorial rain forest... Their descendants are the Pygmies—also called Negrillos, Twa (Batawa), and Twides ...(48)

The little person was not of the ethnic group that inhabited Yam, so we can make one of two assumptions: either (a) Yam may have extended deeper into Africa than the First Cataract; or (b) perhaps the people of Yam had obtained him through trade or barter. Both assumptions imply that the Kemites routinely traded and interacted with the rest of Africa, both in the material and the spiritual realm.

Another name for Lower Nubia was Wawat, believed to have been located between the Sixth and Fifth Afrocentric Cataracts. The time period when the name Wawat was in use is unclear; there is however a textual reference from Dynasty VI in which Uni "secured the assistance of the Chief of Wawat in building wooden barges" (W.Y. Adams 1977, 158). The name Kush has been identified in Pharaonic texts from 2000 B.C.E. About the origins of the name, S. Adams (1981) writes:

> As the geographical name Kush is connected with Kerma and the tumuli clearly show that they were the burials of strong native rulers who had commercial and diplomatic relations with the Hyksos kings in Egypt, it seems more likely that Kerma was the capital of the kingdom of Kush...The existence of this kingdom...is now known from a variety of documentary evidence. (261)

The southern boundaries of Kush are unknown. S. Adams (1981) proposes that "If we accept the hypothesis that the kingdom of Kerma [Kush] stretched from the Third Cataract up to the White Nile, it would have controlled not only the great north-south artery formed by the Nile valley but also the east-west routes from Atlantic Africa to the Red Sea and Indian Ocean. It was therefore well placed to pass on techniques and ideas from Egypt...to the African cultures of these regions" (239).

In 1949, Save-Soderbergh translated an unpublished stela from Buhen that throws light on the question of Kush and its rulers. He interprets it as an " 'autobiography' of an Egyptian serving the free native ruler of Cush" (50). He argues that this stela (and another from that same period) should be dated to the period between Dynasties XIII and XVIII. "In both cases we have 'autobiographies' of Egyptians who served under the free native ruler" (55). Save-

Soderbergh found it "surprising that a free native ruler of Cush should have had Egyptians in his service so short a time after the Egyptian yoke had been thrown off and should have a temple built by an Egyptian at Buhen, the old Egyptian stronghold" (56). He questions his own interpretation: "Now it is true that the *native kinglets* play a certain role in the administration of Nubia even after the reconquest...but is it plausible that they had a position such as implied by these texts?" [emphasis added] (56). Clearly the ancient Egyptian did not have a problem for "Ka starts his biography with emphasizing his loyalty to the ruler of Cush, any prejudice against service in *a foreign country* seems to be excluded" [emphasis added] (53).

The location of Kush at the time of the inscriptions can be determined from Kamose's famous speech made before the reconquest of Kemet after rule by the Hyksos. Save-Soderbergh writes:

> ...[I]n Kamoses's famous speech to his grandees: "To what end am I cognizant of it, this power of mine, when one chieftain is in Avaris and another in Cush, and I sit in league with an Asiatic and a Nubian, every man holding his slice of Egypt..." 'Elephantine is strong,' shows that northern frontier of this free Nubia was at the First Cataract [Afr: Sixth Cataract]. Hence, from a combination of this text with the Buhen stelae, it would seem possible to conclude that one single Nubian ruler dominated the whole of Lower Nubia. (56-57)

It is also possible to conclude, from an African-centered perspective, that there were powerful rulers in Cush before the eighth century. Also, the texts mentioned above suggest that even though the Nubians worked in conjunction with the Hyksos invaders, the relation between Kemet and Cush quickly improved and Egyptians were serving a Cushite king very shortly after the reconquest. This is not the case with Asia, for Egypt's relations with Asia did not progress as smoothly, nor as rapidly. The present work's thesis is that this rapid improvement in the relationship between Kemet and Kush occurred because the two shared common ancestors and had many cultural indices in common.

Nubian history and culture have received greater international attention recently, with major exhibits at numerous museums. In 1978, the Brooklyn Museum opened the first Nubian exhibit in the United States. It was a four-venue exhibit entitled "Africa in Antiquity, the Arts of Ancient Nubia and the Sudan." The University of Pennsylvania Museum on October 10, 1992 opened a traveling exhibit entitled "Ancient Nubia: Egypt's Rival In Africa," which ran through October 1993. The exhibit is traveling to seven sites in the United States and another twenty sites are on the waiting list. The Museum of Fine Arts at Boston opened the first and only permanent gallery in the United States dedicated to the art of ancient Nubia on May 10, 1993. From February 1992 through December 1992, the Oriental Institute Museum in Chicago ran an exhibit entitled "Vanished Kingdoms of the Nile: The Rediscovery of Ancient Nubia." The Royal Ontario Museum at Toronto opened a permanent installation in January of 1993 which the museum hailed as the "first permanent Nubian Gallery in North America" (*KMT: A Modern Journal of Ancient Egypt*, Vol. 3, No. 3, Fall 1992). The Metropolitan Museum of Art in New York City exhibited "The Gold of Meroe" from November 23, 1993 through April 3, 1994. These exhibits demonstrate that an interest in Nubia, as a entity separate from its relationship to Egypt, is on the rise.

Afrocentric scholars influenced this change of perspective on Nubia. In an article in *Newsweek* for October 19, 1992, the writers acknowledged this influence:

> ...scholars are rethinking the conventional views of Nubia. *The revisionism, spurred by the Afrocentrism movement among classics scholars*, coincides with a new exhibit, "Ancient Nubia: Egypt's Rival in Africa," which opened last week at the University

Museum of Archeology at the University of Pennsylvania. (60)

This article reveals that Afrocentricity is causing a paradigm shift with respect to African peoples among the most Eurocentric of scholarly circles.

Cheikh Anta Diop was an African-centered scholar who excelled in many disciplines, including history, linguistics, physics, mathematics, and cultural and physical anthropology. Diop was born on December 29, 1923 in Dioubel, Senegal. He died in 1986. He was the director and founder of the radiocarbon laboratory of the Institut Francais d'Afrique Noire at Dakar. However, his most outstanding legacy was his meticulous scholarship. In 1966, at the first World Festival of Negro Arts, he and W.E.B. DuBois were awarded recognition as the writers who had the greatest influence on Black thought in the twentieth century. His earned degrees, Doctor of Letters and qualifications in physics, were the product of fierce determination. He had to rewrite his dissertation three times before it was accepted by the University of Paris. That is because he chose a controversial subject matter—the African origins of ancient Egypt. This bold, brave, and indefatigable spirit was his hallmark throughout his career.

This intrepid spirit certainly was useful when Diop participated in the UNESCO International Scientific Committee of the Drafting of a General History of Africa. He was part of the Symposium on the Peopling of Ancient Egypt (Mokhtar 1981, 58). Challenged aggressively by scholars from all over the world, he and his colleague, Theophile Obenga, presented copious evidence to support their thesis that Ancient Egypt was a Black civilization. Their presentation led to lively discussions and remonstrations. The outcome was that African historiography will never be the same. It will no longer be business as usual, that is, written by those who do not have the interests of Africans at the center of their analysis. Diop may not have changed world opinion, but he and Obenga put the African-centered perspective of African history on the international agenda.

In *The African Origin Of Civilization: Myth or Reality?* ([1955] 1974) Diop provides the reader with evidence that ancient Egypt was a Negro civilization. The use of the word "Negro" was to connect ancient Egypt with other African civilizations. Diop considered this a key position from which to view African history because "The history of Black Africa will remain suspended in air and cannot be written correctly until African historians dare to connect it with the history of Egypt" (xiv). Diop's book is divided into thirteen chapters; in Chapter VII, he presents several cultural indices supporting a Negro origin of Ancient Egypt: totemism, kingship, matriarchy, circumcision, cosmogony, social organization, and languages. In the present work, we will utilize and expand upon four of the categories to analyze the culture of Kush.

The eight categories in Diop's Chapter VII are totemism, circumcision, divine kingship, cosmogony, social organization, matriarchy, kinship, and languages. We will focus on totemism, divine kingship, cosmogony, and matriarchy. The remaining four categories are valid to the issue of commonalities of African culture, however the nature of the history of the culture of Kush does not provide enough evidence to assess these.

NOTES

1. Barksdale, Richard and Kenneth Kinnamon, eds., *Black Writers of America: A Comprehensive Anthology* (New York: The Macmillan Co., 1972).

2. Imhotep was the chief advisor to the Pharaoh Djoser, a king of the third Dynasty. He was an architect, priest, physician, writer of proverbs, and builder of the first pyramid (the Step Pyramid). After his death, he was worshipped as a demigod by the ancient Egyptians His fame was widespread and he was also worshipped by the Greeks and the Phoenicians.

3. "Pygmy" is a name reflective of the perspective of Europeans. It derives from the Greek word *pygme*, meaning "half an arm's length." They are not short by their own standards. A recent article in *National Geographic Magazine* states that the term is pejorative, "yet the name has stuck to these, the world's shortest people" (July 1995). Even in these times of so-called political correctness, old ways still prevail.

CHAPTER TWO

CLEARING A MUDDLED PERSPECTIVE

"African Civilization Not African" Literature

Current writings about Nubia perpetuate the failure to place the African Kingdom of Kush *in* Africa. Michael Botwinick, the Director of The Brooklyn Museum, in his foreword to *Africa In Antiquity: The Arts of Ancient Nubia and the Sudan* (1978), attempts to place Nubia for his readers by characterizing it as "*neither Egyptian nor African*, yet often both...Throughout recorded history it lies at the outer edge, first of the ancient world, then at the edge of the Classical world...*contact and transfer point between Africa and...Ancient Egypt...*" [emphasis added] (9). This backhanded reference to Nubia being "sometimes" African is assumed to be less Eurocentric than past writings on this subject. Current literature on Kush, however, still serves the same purpose as previously: to valorize the superiority of Europe.

Archeological excavations provide useful material about Kush even though its internal documents have not been interpreted. The indigenous script is Meroitic. The basic components of the language are known. There are twenty-three letters, four vowels, groups of dots used as word-dividers, purely numerical signs, metrical signs, some ideographic symbols, and some evidence of a calendar. The equivalence of the hieroglyphic alphabet and the cursive Meriotic alphabet is somewhat determined. The phonetic values have been equated with Kemetic hieroglyphic and demotic scripts (Theophile Obenga, Temple University lecture, 1993). Greek similarities are plentiful.

The script can be read phonetically, but the meaning of the words is unknown. The deciphering has been hindered by the lack of a significant bilingual key, such as the Rosetta Stone. Lepsius, an archeologist, did find during his excavations in Wad Benage an engraving of a king and queen which contained cartouches with their names written in Meroitic character above them and in Egyptian on the side. These small but important bilingual keys have provided the "starting point of all subsequent investigations into hieroglyphic writing of the Meroites" (Griffith 1912, 68). The written records of the kings of the 25th Dynasty in the *mdu neter* or hieroglyphics provide internal documents that will be used in this book.

Most of what is known about Kush is inferred from topologies or groupings of similar types of monuments and excavations. However, excavations are very destructive. Once an area has been excavated, it has been totally destroyed. In the case of Kush, the Aswan High Dam project has left much of what was once Kush under water. Lower Nubia is now under Lake Nasser. One must then rely on archeological reports of findings. These reports then become primary source documents. The present work will use the information contained in these archeological reports; however, unlike past analyses this work will interpret those reports within an Afrocentric paradigm.

Graham Connah's *African Civilizations—Precolonial Cities and States in Tropical Africa: An Archeological Perspective* (1987) postulates that so-called tropical Africa "attained cultural complexity of a high order" (ix). He bases his claim on the interpretation of material evidence from excavations. He further supports it with illustrations, photographs, and references from the existing literature on the subject. Connah proposes that to fully understand Africa's past, one must use the discipline of archeology "in order to reconstruct" (2) the past. He admits that one disadvantage of archeology is that the evidence is always only part of the whole picture. Archeological maps, he asserts, show the distribution of research done, not the evidence that is potentially available. Yet, he does not state how the value system of the person doing the reconstruction affects the whole field of archeology. He presents case studies of various societies defined by sectioning off Africa into west, east and southern Africa, but excluding Egypt. This exclusion continues "the *unfortunate*...practice of beheading the African continent, which has in recent years become identified by the use of the phrase 'sub-Saharan'" [emphasis added] (21). However, he himself does this for what he believes are "good reasons" (21). The purpose of his book, he declares, is to examine the formation of cities and states in "black Africa" (21) and in his opinion Egypt is not in so-called black Africa. He places Egypt in the Mediterranean.

The cities of the middle Nile are defined as a cul-de-sac or corridor in Africa. Relying on Adams' *Nubia: Corridor To Africa* (1977) as his primary source of information, Connah locates Nubia in "the transition zone, *between the civilized world and Africa*" (24). The civilized world to which he refers is Egypt and other so-called Mediterranean countries. Furthermore, he states that the importance of this corridor is that it was the only "dependable route across the great *barrier* of the Sahara Desert. The African interior contained resources much coveted by this *outside* world: gold, ivory, slaves" [emphasis added] (25).

Connah does credit Nubia with being the first in so-called tropical Africa to form cities and states, in spite of a so-called extreme environment. Yet, in his analysis, the position of Nubia *vis-à-vis* Egypt is an example of the "age-old interchange between developed and underdeveloped world: manufactures for raw materials" (61). This perspective typifies the past and current state of the writings about Nubia and Kemet. In the passage just cited, he separates Egypt and Nubia into developed and underdeveloped worlds, and then assigns positive and negative values to the parts, with Egypt having more positive value as the 'developed' world. This is a common practice among Europeans that can be seen in any newspaper or periodical today, in any comparison between African and Western countries.

The same world-view is evident in historiography concerning Kush. Even though Connah's interpretations of Nile Valley civilizations are suspect, still, his illustrations and references are helpful. The evidence that he adduces to support his central claim—that this part of Africa produced complex societies—is also useful.

Connah, like all social scientists, is his own primary instrument of analysis. He has been acculturated to a Eurocentric world-view which has caused him to misunderstand the culture of the people whom he has spent a great deal of his life studying. For example, in examining the Nubians he states that at one time scholars believed that the "ideas of divine kingship [spread] from the Nile to as far away as West Africa" (65). He discounts this because of lack of archeological evidence and concludes that Nubia had "very little influence on the rest of Africa" (65). Yet, again and again, in each society he examines, the concept of the priest/ruler appears, a concept that is clearly evident first in Kush and then Kemet (Williams 1980). Connah fails to acknowledge commonalities.

This failure to see what Cheikh Anta Diop refers to as the "cultural unity" of Africa (1963) also hinders Connah when he views the Sahara as a barrier. The Sahara was not insurmountable for African people. There is evidence of various animals and plant life left by former residents of the Sahara in the form of very elaborate rock drawings. These drawings indicate that it was once a fertile environment (Davidson 1966a, 11). Africans have crossed, lived and traded in the Sahara for millennia. It may have been an inconvenience, but it has not been a barrier, certainly, no more a barrier than the Mediterranean Sea. The Sahara did not begin to dry up until 2500 B.C.E. People began to move out around 2000 B.C.E. Afterward there is evidence that carts and chariots drawn by donkeys and horses were used to cross the Sahara between North and West Africa around 1000 B.C.E. and camels from 100 B.C.E. until the present day (11).

Connah and other archaeologists use terms such as "animism," "precolonial," "prehistory," "Black Africa," and "sub-Saharan Africa," which tend to devalue the culture of African people. The end result is that, although he aims to be a trail blazer, Connah still stands outside of Africa and ultimately is travelling down the same old road.

William Adams' *Nubia: Corridor to Africa* (1977) is regarded as the seminal book on Nubia. He spent seven years in Nubia (1959-66) directing the archeological salvage campaign for UNESCO and the Sudan Antiquities Service. He is by far the most quoted authority on Nubian history, yet he too places Nubia outside of both the civilized world *and* so-called Black Africa.

> ...the Nubians undoubtedly found the role of black man in a white man's world [Kemet] as detrimental as have all black races everywhere...they were able to absorb a good deal of civilization of their neighbors, and in so doing *to detach themselves from the wholly primitive world of black Africa* [emphasis added]...Nubia became...*the* transition zone [emphasis original], between the civilized world and Africa...[they] became in every sense *middle men—racially and culturally as well as economically* [emphasis added]. (20)

Adams creates wholly new concepts—"transition zone" and "racial and cultural middle-men"—in which to place Nubia, but not without continuing to affirm the superiority of Europeans. The "transition-zone" concept posits the superiority of Europe and inferiority of Africa. His book uses less blatantly racist terms than in the past; however, it is firmly entrenched in an Eurohegemonic and Eurocentric world view.

The denial of the African foundation of Kemet is at work in Adams' writings whenever the influence of Kemet on Nubia is viewed as a non-African influence:

> If I may sum up the definition of Nubia in a few words...[it] is occupied by peoples African in origin and speech *but strongly influenced by Egyptian and Mediterranean culture* [emphasis added]. (21)

The assumption that Egypt is not African is implicit in this passage. This concept is so embedded in the foundations of Egyptology that no explanation is given or even expected as to *why* Egypt is not African; it is part of the assumed knowledge base.

The Issue of Race

> Until the philosophy which holds
> One race superior and another inferior
> Is finally and permanently discredited
> And abandoned
> Until the color of a man skin
> Is of no more significance than
> The color of his eyes...
>
> --Bob Marley, "War,"
> *Rastaman Vibration*[1]

Adams recounts how the terms in use today to classify periods of Nubian history came into being. This also demonstrates how the analysis of skeletal remains has been key to the Eurocentric reconstruction of Nubian history. All archeological remains have to be interpreted and these Nubian remains were interpreted based on the assumed supremacy of Europe. The classification of Nubian chronology into 'A-Group', 'B-Group', 'C-Group', and 'X-Group' was determined by the degree of so-called Negro characteristics of the exhumed skeletons. The amount analyzed was approximately fifteen to twenty percent of the exhumed skeletons because most of them were in very poor condition. This system was developed and solidified in 1907-08 and, even though the philosophical underpinnings have been challenged, it continues in use today. Adams enlightens us about the process:

> Elliot Smith and Derry had *no difficulty recognizing significant racial differences* among the skeletons from the various Nubian grave types. The people of the 'A-Group' they believed to be identical with the pre-dynastic Egyptians, while in the 'B-Group' they perceived a *much stronger Negro strain*. This element was still believed to be present, although much diluted, in the 'C-Group'...The same racial amalgam was seen in the subsequent Nubian populations down to the 'X-Group', when there is a *second heavy Negro infusion*. [emphasis mine] (91)

Craniologist Elliot Smith's opinion of alleged "negro blood" is evident in his statement that "the *smallest infusion of Negro-blood immediately manifests itself in a dulling of initiative and a 'drag' on the further development of the arts of civilization*" [emphasis added] (92).

Smith, however, not only divided the Nubians from the ancient Egyptians, he explained the difference in the cultures in the following manner:

> The recently acquired knowledge...has familiarized us with *an epoch that lasted until about 2800 B.C., when Egypt and Lower Nubia were occupied by one uniform population in the same stage of culture*...[T]his information was interpreted as

> meaning that while Egypt advanced with rapid strides...Nubia...fell away from the standard of knowledge and skill she had possessed before the time of the Pyramid builders...
>
> ...[A] more detailed study...has convinced me that a slightly different explanation must be found to account for the known facts.
>
> ...no _pure_ Negroes were found amongst the remains of these people buried in Nubia, during the Ancient Empire...it was the mongrel population and not the Negro element only that came north into Nubia. The difference in culture was not the result of a falling away from a higher standard, but was due...to the fact that the less favorably placed kinsmen of the Proto-Egyptians had not kept pace with them in their acquirement of a higher civilization. (Smith 1911, 66-68)

The variations in culture between the Kemites and the Nubians are ranked according to Eurocentric determinants of civilization and progress. Smith's hypotheses are built around racial differences between the Nubians and Kemites.

> ...[O]nly weaker brethren were left in Nubia; and these feeble folk were unable to resist the immigration of Negroes, who came up from south, intermingled with them, and dragged down their cultural attainments to a lower plane [emphasis added]. (67)

Thus it is Smith's belief that there are distinct racial and cultural differences between the peoples of Kemet and of Kush and that these differences can be explained by the inability of the Nubians to resist the infusion of so-called

Negroes, who pulled their culture down. The negative view of so-called Negroes in this hypothesis is transparent.

G. Elliot Smith (1911) did face challenges to his hypotheses. He voiced his concern that respected Europeans such as Volney and Ripley "expressed the belief that the Ancient Egyptians were Negroes, or at least strongly Negroid" (30). He answered such "beliefs" with "science," stating that "it was not until the detailed investigation of the human remains found in Nubia during the last four years was undertaken that the full significance of the Egyptian remains began to emerge with any clearness" (39). Examples of Smith's level of clarity have already been cited, above (36).

Another challenge—which Smith and others have not faced—is the testimony of the ancient Egyptians themselves:

> [I]t is not without significance that the Ancient Egyptians were accustomed to speak of the Land of Punt as their homeland.... There must have been some kind of intercourse between Egypt and the Somali region ...(76)

Smith simply asserts that the Puntites were Hamites and once again the Hamitic myth is used to fill in gaps of logic in the discussion of race and the Nile Valley.

The racial basis of this classification has been challenged, and yet the theory still survives. Batrawi, who was in charge of the anatomical material of the Second Archeological Survey of Nubia (1929-1934), found that "no marked differences...and no appreciable change in the variabilities of the ancient male Nubian populations are noticeable as we pass from any group to the one immediately following it in chronological order" (Batrawi 1945, 86). He also found a similar lack of difference in the female series. In a comparison of crania from Africa and Britain, he determined that "The Egyptian and Palestinian series are too few to encourage generalization, but it may be noted that, on the scale considered, the Nubian series are much closer to the Egyptian and Palestinian than these are to the British series" (89). These findings, even though confirmed by other studies (Mukherjee, Rao and Trevor 1955), have been ignored to this day. This is an example of what C.T. Keto has referred to as "the tyranny of evidence." The position of Elliot Smith as *the* Nubian racial expert was so strong that Batrawi was "reluctant to challenge his historical theories even while he disputed their empirical foundation" (W. Adams 1977, 92). Batrawi eventually did challenge these views a decade later, in 1946, when he wrote that "The literature dealing with the *racial history of Egypt and Nubia provides an outstanding example of the danger of assessing biological relationships from cultural evidence*" [emphasis added] (131).

The "multi-racial history" of Nubia can still be seen in the following passage. The major racial difference is conjectured to be between Lower Nubia, called Wawat, and Upper Nubia, referred to as Kush. In his *Egypt in Nubia* (1965), Emery states:

> As far as can be ascertained on the available archeological evidence, the peoples of Wawat and Kush, although related, were *racially distinct*. This evidence suggests that the inhabitants of Wawat were generally an unwarlike people while the people of Kush were of fighting stock [emphasis added]. (16)

Emery bases his racial evidence solely on fighting abilities. Emery continues "As in ancient times, the Nubian of today is racially distinct from the Egyptian...they remain to a large extent a race apart" (17). Since the Egyptians of today are largely descendants of the Islamic Arabic conquerors, not of the Kemetic people of antiquity, this is a spurious argument.

Reisner designates the Wawat as a "tribe" that lived between Dongola and Assuan. He informs us that "From ...inscriptions it appears that the country southward of Assuan was inhabited by a series of tribes whom the

Egyptians designated as negroes....Our present evidence is that they were not true negroes" (Reisner 1918, I, 12-13). Again, we find the presumption of who *is* and who *is not* a "true negro" as a method of separating African peoples.

Adams uses a Eurocentric paradigm that cloaks its intentions with liberal semantics. He discounts the racist implications of these classifications. He allows that "Nubia has always had an African or quasi-African population different from that of Egypt, and knowing this leaves us *no wiser about the political, social, or cultural history of the country*" [emphasis added] (95). Thus, even though Nubia is in Africa, for Adams this has no cultural implications.

In 1920, Dr. Hermann Junker, an archeologist, wrote an article in *The Journal of Egyptian Archeology* entitled "The First Appearance of the Negroes in History." He began by correcting what he called a fallacy: "According to the popular conceptions Africa is the Black continent, the domain of the Negroes, in which other races play only a quite subordinate part. Neither for the present time, however, nor as regards antiquity does this view correspond to the facts" (16). The facts as he views them are that Africa has been equally shared by the so-called Negroes and the so-called "Hamites." He does not define what constitutes a Hamite, but the commonly held theory is that they were 'dark skinned white people.' Bruce Trigger, an archeologist, writes that the "Hamitic hypothesis" speculated that the Hamites were "pictured as being tall, light-skinned pastoralists who were 'better armed as well as quicker-witted than the dark agricultural Negroes' ...These qualities permitted the Hamites to push south and replace or establish themselves as a ruling class amongst the indigenous Blacks" (1978, 28).

There are two reasons why Junker's article is important: (1) in it he sought to prove that the Nubians are not the first so-called Negroes to appear in history because they were not black; (2) it demonstrates how the Western academy has not been purged of its racist, Eurocentric, and ethnocentric point of view in as much as the article is frequently used as a scholarly reference, and Junker is highly regarded by the Western academy as a preeminent authority on the race of the Egyptians and Nubians. In *Egypt Before The Pharaohs* (1979) by Michael A. Hoffman, an entire chapter is devoted to "Father Junker":

> Hermann Junker was the model of a successful German university professor.... Between 1908 and 1911 he undertook a mission to Nubia for the Prussian Academy of Science as part of an effort to rescue monuments threatened by the expansion of the ten-year old Aswan dam. Between 1912 and 1929, he dug at Giza...adding immensely to our knowledge of the culture of the Old Kingdom...he accommodated himself to the Nazi government. (198-9)

Armed with these credentials and archeological remains from his excavations, Junker made well-received pronouncements about Nubian and Kemetic culture:

> Now, that an attempt should be made to throw some light on the history of the Blacks from the Egyptological side needs no justification. For Egypt is a part of Africa, and has the oldest history available to us... No more need to be recalled here that the prehistoric skeletons...[excavated] in Upper Egypt *Elliot Smith assumes 2% with negroid traits, but it is practically certain that this state of things is to be explained otherwise than by the immigration of Negroes dwelling near by* [emphasis mine]. (122-123)

The reason he believes that they cannot have migrated from Nubia is that:

> They certainly cannot have entered gradually from the south through Nubia: for...*neither pure nor hybrid Negroes* appear during the prehistoric period, and even in the subse-

> quent A-period down to the Second Dynasty...It should be remembered that both in Nubia and at Nag'ed-Der *the appearance of somewhat negroid traits in isolated individuals is very far from implying any connection, whether direct or indirect with full Negroes*....Should the existence of a pure Negro at Nag'ed-Der really be demonstrated...he certainly arrived there by way of trade, and *his tribe must have dwelt far away.* [emphasis mine] (123)

Junker also criticized a "fable convenue among historians, and many anthropologists" (123), namely, that "the history of the Negroes began as far back as circa 3000 B.C.E., and we are able to follow the fortunes of their northernmost representatives from that time onwards uninterruptedly" (124). This, he speculates, is completely untrue. He bases his argument on his interpretation of the material evidence from his excavations. According to Junker, "[r]epresentations of Negroes are wholly absent in the Old Kingdom" (124). Also, he translates the word "*nhsyw*" to mean Hamites. The interpretation of this word is essential to the placement of African people in the Nile Valley. According to Junker, the so-called Negro appears in history in the New Kingdom of Kemet when "a considerable *accretion of Negroes* and negroid elements has to be reckoned with in Nubia" [emphasis added] (130).

It could be said that Junker was writing during a time less enlightened than today. However, African history in general and Nubian history in particular has still not been purged of this world-view. The words have changed but the goal of maintaining the supremacy of Europe has not. Archeologist Bruce Trigger, in his 1978 article "Nubian, Negro, Black, Nilotic?" still quotes Junker as an expert on interpreting Nubian phenotypes:

> Artistic representations also suggest a regional continuity in physical type. Junker (1921) was the first to note that during the

Old and Middle Kingdoms, when direct Egyptian contacts appear not to have extended much farther south than the Third Cataract, only Nubian types were portrayed by Egyptian artists...(31).

Trigger, in effect, pasteurizes Junker's analysis. Junker had based his statements on some vague definition of who "possess[es] the specific Negro character" (Junker 1921, 124). Junker even states the reddish color of the people on the reliefs was only a convention and had no relationship to their actual coloring.

Trigger, in an attempt to redefine the discourse on the people of the Nile Valley, discounts the whole notion of race. He quotes Diop in this attempt to devalue the concept of race. Trigger writes "As Diop (1962, 461) has observed, the Platonic ideal of pure races became so compelling that it resulted in all real peoples (except perhaps those of one's own nationality) being viewed as belonging to false races" (26). Diop has written extensively on the issue of the so-called pure Negro. In other words, he has challenged scholars, like Trigger, who base their arguments on vague definitions of so-called Negroes. Diop, whose view is key to the present work, addresses the issue quite forthrightly:

> Anthropologists have invented the ingenious convenient fictional notion of the 'true Negro' which allows them to consider, if need be all the real Negroes on earth as fake Negroes, more or less approaching a kind of Platonic archetype, without ever attaining it. Thus African history is full of Negroids, Hamites, semi-Hamites, Neo-Hamitics, Ethiopiods, Sabeans, even Caucasoids! ([1955] 1974, 274)

Trigger may attempt to deflect the issue of race by making it a non-issue; however, other writers in the same anthology, *Africa in Antiquity: The Arts of Ancient Nubia and the Sudan* (1978), do not. One of the writers in the anthology, archeologist Jean Leclant, for example, writes concerning his interpretation of the so-called role of Africans in Kemetic society:

> Monuments of the New Kingdom frequently picture the pharaoh smiting his fettered enemies...among them, *the Negro, symbol of the south, is easily recognizable*...Although *the Negro was pictured among Egypt's traditional enemies from earliest times*, in the New Kingdom such representations of royal conquests become more abundant. The heads of black captives occur on the bases of statues, on the planks of ships, on the body of the pharaoh's chariot. Tutankhamen's walking sticks permitted the head of Negroes to trail in the dust.... [emphasis added] (69)

This is a common problem with Eurocentric archeology and historiography. Practitioners ostensibly deny the significance of race when they are discussing the specific issue of the race of the Kemites and/or the Kushites; yet, in all other aspects of their discourse, they use the very racial concepts whose existence they deny. Leclant identifies the specific characteristics of so-called Negroes that make them so "easily recognizable." What criteria, for example, is he using to distinguish these so-called Negroid characteristics from those of Cheops or Amunhotep III or the woman in the Royal Hairdressing Scene? (*Ancient Egyptian Art in the Brooklyn Museum* 9,44 (1989), 17). Moreover, in regard to the aforementioned anthology, Leclant leaves the uninformed reader with the impression, that the only relationship the rulers of Kemet had with people of the south was that of conqueror and conquered. This negates most of the history of Kush and denies the historical record. During a visit to Hatshepsut's temple in the valley of the kings, this writer observed painted on the walls depictions of trade between Punt and Kemet. This is an indication of positive commercial relationships between Kemet and other parts of Africa. It is data pertinent to the understanding of African history.

In the discussions that follow I will assume that the people of the Nile Valley are of indigenous African ancestry, not Mediterranean. Neither the word Negro nor the word Negroid will be used to describe them because these words are rooted in the *maafa* of enslavement (Moore [1960], 1992). Moore chronicles the first use of the word "negro." He cites the *Chronicle of the Discovery and Conquest of Guinea* by Gomes Eannes Azurara (1453). In this chronicle, Azurara describes how Dinnis Fernandes Diaz "passed the land of the Moors and arrived in the land of the blacks, that is called Guinea. But when the *negroes* saw that those in the ship were men, they made haste to flee...but because our men had a better opportunity than before, they captured them, and these were the first to be taken by Christians in their own land..." [emphasis added] (38). Moore provides additional enlightenment in the following passage:

> If Azurara's Chronicle [in which the first written use of the word appears] was completed in 1453 as stated, then it is certain that the terms "negro" and "negroes" were in use in Portugal by the date of 1453. Other statements in this Chronicle...also point to the use of the term "negroes" even as early as 1443. This term "negroes" was then used with a new and specific meaning as a name or designation particularly applied to African slaves....

From that period onward, this name "negroes" was connected to and loaded with vicious and degrading notions of class, "race," and color prejudice. In this way the black color and other physical features of African slaves were identified in the mind of people generally with ugliness, repulsion, and baseness. By this name "negros," African slaves were thereby branded as bestial and savage, innately inferior, fit by nature only for slavery, and indeed ordained by God himself for perpetual slavery. (40)

The word Negro has never had a definite meaning from the time of its first usage to the current times. Asante (1990) elucidates the problem with referring to African people as Negroes:

> There is no ethnic group in Africa that calls itself negro or its language negro. *The term is preeminently a creation of the European mind to refer to any African group or people who correspond to a certain negative image of culture.* The term is meaningless in reality but has become a useful word for those who would serve a political purpose by the term. Thus, the word "negro" is used by white writers to obfuscate...[emphasis added]. (132)

Moore quotes R.N. Cust in *Modern Languages of Africa* (1833) on the problem which is still with us today:

> It is often asked what Races are Negro, as the meaning of the term is not well defined. The word is not a National appellation, but denotes a physical type, of which the tribes in North Guinea are the representatives. When these characteristics are not all present, the race is not "Negro," though black and woolly-haired. (132)

The issue of the so-called Hamites is an essential aspect of the question of the race of the Nubians. Even though the actual term Hamite is little used today, I contend that the underlying concept is still very much alive. Anthropologist Charles Gabriel Seligman wrote extensively about Hamites in his book *Races of Africa* ([1930] 1957). It is his work that provided the foundation of the Hamitic concept. Seligman makes a point of informing his readers that the Hamites and the Semites have a common origin. Africa, in his world-view, is inhabited by five races: in typical Eurocentric manner, he lists them in hierarchal order:

> ...[T]he greatest divisions of mankind inhabiting Africa, *its principal races from the standpoint of the distinctness of each from the other and their importance*, are as follows:
> (1) Hamites
> (2) Semites
> (3) Negroes
> (4) Bushman
> (4a) Hottetots
> (5) Negrillos
> (Seligman 1957, 6)

Not only are the Hamites on the top, he also credits them with being "the great civilizing force of black Africa"(10). Needless to say, these so-called Hamites are related to Europeans. He sees a distinct separation in Africa, as do modern Eurocentric writers (Connah, 1987). The *term* "sub-Sahara" had not yet been developed, but the *concept* of the division of Africa was very much alive. Seligman postulates that "the Sahara in the main separates Negroland from the Mediterranean populations" (10). Seligman even dedicates a chapter to describing the so-called "true Negro." He describes them for his readers:

> the...Negro...almost everywhere characterized by their dark skin and spiralled hair....the term "Negro" includes at least three huge groups, each with its peculiar characteristics....The true Negro is mainly confined to the neighborhood of the Guinea coast....The rest of Negro Africa consists of Negroes hamiticized to a varying extent: on the one hand Bantu, on the other the Nilotes and "Nilo-Hamites." [emphasis added] (42-43)

Seligman fails to see Africa in holistic terms. He forthrightly subdivides the so-called Hamites:

> (1) *The Eastern Hamites comprise the ancient and modern Egyptians (in the latter case recognizing the infusion of foreign blood in the upper classes), the Beja, the Berberines (Barbara or Nubians)*, the Galla, the Somali, the Danakil, and, though mixed with Semites and Negroes, most Ethiopians. (2) The Northern Hamites include the Berbers of Cyrenaica, Tripolitania, Tunisia, and Algeria (often conventionally distinguished as Libyans), the Berbers of Morocco, the Tuareg and Tibu of the Sahara, the Fula of Nigeria, and the extinct Guanche of the Canary Islands. [emphasis added] (86)

It was this conception of Hamites that allowed Eurocentric scholars to place the people of the Nile Valley in a category which separates them from the rest of Africa. It also allowed these scholars to rank the peoples of Africa in hierarchial order. The Hamitic concept was indispensable to the process of the beheading of Africa.

Seligman describes the Nubians in terms which more reflect his racism than the world-view of the ancient Egyptians:

> The stele at Semma near the cataract reads: '*Southern boundary*, made in the year 8, under the majesty of the King of Upper and Lower Egypt, Khekure (Sesotris III) who is given life for ever and ever; *in order to prevent that any Negro should cross it, by water or land, with a ship (or) any herds of the Negroes; except a Negro who shall come to do trading* in Iken or with a commission. Every good thing shall be done with them, *but without allowing a ship of the Negroes*

> *to pass by Heh, going downstream, for ever'*
> [emphasis added]. (97-98)

The key to this passage rests in the transliteration of the word '*nehsi.*' Eurocentric scholars, consistent with a racist, ethnocentric, and hegemonic world-view, have consistently translated it to mean 'negro.' When they have done so, as in this passage, the term has carried with it all of the modern connotations of denigrated people. '*Nehsi*' is, however, a geographical term, meaning simply "someone from the south." The Kemites had an ideogram for black '*Kmt*;' had they wanted to designate the people from the south as black, (the etymology of the word negro), they would have used it. The ancient Egyptians reserved the term black or '*kam-t*' to describe their own country and themselves as *Kammau*, or black people (Budge [1920] 1978, 787).

In spite of Seligman's interpretation of the Egyptian text in which he states that the ancient Egyptians refer to the Nubians as 'negroes,' Seligman himself classifies them as predominantly Hamitic:

> [S]ome 3,000 years B.C. Nubia was inhabited by a people similar to the predynastic Egyptians, with a civilization essentially resembling that of the latter, if rather less advanced...we can trace the gradual ebb and flow of influence from the north.... Hence there arose in Nubia a hybrid population, blending the characters of Egyptian, Negro, and Beja, and it is this type...which has in the main persisted in Nubia to the present day....(98-99)

Seligman is able, thanks to the contrived concept of Hamite, to classify the Nubians as different from African people who live south of the Sahara. Moreover, even though he classifies both the Nubians and Egyptians as Hamites, he ranks the ancient Egyptians as culturally superior. Faced with evidence of cultural commonalities between predynastic Egyptians and the Nubians, he can discern only separations and hierarchies. This "logic" is seen repeatedly in Eurocentric scholarship.

In the present study, however, the people of Kemet and Kush will be referred to as *African* people, and their ancestors as the *original* African people. They were not direct descendants of conquerors. The term "African people," moreover, will not be a narrowly descriptive one. African people are the most diverse human group because people of African descent have the oldest gene pool. Their genes have had more time to diversify (*Newsweek*, 1988, 46-52; *The New York Times*, July 27, 1993, c-1). Thus, African people will be assumed to be very phenotypically diverse. Their skin can range from various shades of brown to ebony black; their hair from straight to kinky and their noses from broad to straight. However, they are all African people. This term will not be classified into hierarchial rankings. Kemet will be considered the classical civilization of Africa because of its antiquity; its authenticity (that is, Africans living on their own terms); the ubiquity of its documents; the level of its achievements; its relevance to other Africans; and its contribution to world civilization (Maulana Karenga, Lecture, Temple University, February 20, 1993). The Nile Valley is important to an understanding of the rest of Africa, but it is not necessarily superior to other African civilizations.

In order to define what is meant by the term "African people," Diop's definition will be used:

> There are two variants of the black race:
> (a) straight-haired, represented in Asia by the Darvidians and in Africa by the Nubians and the Tubbou or Tedda, all three with jet-black skins:
> (b) the kinky-haired blacks of the Equatorial regions. Both types entered into the composition of the Egyptian population. (1981, 34)

"Meroe Not An African Culture" Literature

Peter L. Shinnie is considered by most Eurocentric scholars to be the foremost expert on Meroe. He was a Professor of Archeology at the University of Ghana from 1958 to 1966 and in 1967 he was Professor of Archeology at the University of Khartoum in the Sudan. He was also part of the UNESCO Aswan salvage campaign (*Meroe: A Civilization of the Sudan*, 1967). Shinnie places Meroe in Africa, but always hesitates in defining Meroites as racially or culturally African. This is his analysis of Meroitic art forms:

> This obviously indigenous element might well be called 'African' and so in a sense it is, since *Meroe is a part of Africa; but* the term is somewhat misleading since it suggests a relationship with art forms of sub-Saharan Africa as they are known today, the art which springs to mind when Africa is mentioned. It is hard to find any connection between the art of Meroe and that of parts further south....[emphasis mine] (101)

Shinnie's theory concerning the race of the Meroites falls under Diop's indictment of anthropologists trying to reach a Platonic archetype of a so-called Negro:

> The many representations of royal persons do not greatly help, though African features can be inferred in some cases...but three skulls found in the tomb of King Amanitenmemide have been studied; of those *one was said to be of Mediterranean type whilst the other two were faintly negroid. Nubia...is today inhabited by a predominately brown-skinned people of aquiline features having in varying degrees an admixture of Negro*, and there is no

reason to suppose that the ancient population were very different [emphasis added]. (155)

Shinnie is willing to place Meroe geographically *in* Africa but he is unwilling to identify the Meroitic people or culture *as* African. I will utilize information from his book after placing this information within an Afrocentric paradigm.

Archeologist Margaret Shinnie, wife of Peter Shinnie and his assistant in his field work in the Sudan, places the Kushites in Africa. However, this placement, in her analysis, separates them from the Kemites because she does not place Kemet in Africa. Thus, even though she is able to locate Kush in Africa, her world-view is still limited by what Marimba Ani (1993) has referred to as *utamawazo,* that is, culturally structured thought (xxv). Ani elaborates on how important *utamawazo* is to hegemonic behavior of Europeans:

> The process of dichotimization in the European *utamawazo* is of great significance ....The *utamaroho*, which needs to control, is dependent on the antagonistic oppositions presented by the cognitive style (*utamawazo*) of the cultural myth (mythoform). Realities are split, then evaluated, so that one part is "better", which mandates its controlling function [emphasis original]. (33)

Let us examine how Margaret Shinnie describes the Kushites in her book on *Ancient African Kingdoms* (1970):

> First of all, we must notice that the Kushites were an African people....*In their wall painting, the Egyptians showed the Kushites as having dark skins in contrast to their own lighter ones, and sometimes drew their hair differently....The Kushites were the first truly African people to achieve a position of power and importance and to win respect of*

the civilized world as it was at that time. [emphasis added] (39)

Not only is Margaret Shinnie unable to maintain a holistic view of Africa; once again we see the positive valorization of Kush merely because it was respected by the so-called civilized world.

The placement of Meroe *geographically within* Africa, yet *culturally outside* of Africa, is also seen in the writings of Steffen Wenig, editor of *Africa in Antiquity: The Arts of Nubia and the Sudan, Volume II* (1978). This two-volume book is a catalogue published in conjunction with an exhibit of the same name organized by the Brooklyn Museum. The art in this book is, in the opinion of the present researcher, visually similar to other art forms in Africa. The published comments in the aforementioned catalogue (concerning an inlaid cosmetic container) bespeak a reluctance on the part of the Brooklyn Museum and their collaborators, the International Council of Museums, to place Meroe culturally in Africa:

> [t]his cosmetic container...is perhaps a typical African element of decoration, but *the complex problem of possible African influence on Meroitic art has been too little investigated for more to be said.*(265-6)

Commonalities among African people are viewed as problematic by the organizers of this major exhibit of art from Meroe and other parts of Nubia. Not only do the organizers fail to locate Meroe *in* Africa, they are hesitant to declare any influence by Africa on Meroe. I, on the other hand, *assume* that African people have interrelated since very ancient times. This assumption is essential to a holistic understanding of Meroitic, Napatan, and Kemetic culture.

At present, most of the chronology of Nubia has been reconstructed from information gathered from excavations of the largest group of pyramids anywhere in the world. The presence, quantity, and quality of these pyramids in Kush provide evidence that this was a state society. Archeologist Bruce Trigger, in his article "Monumental Architecture: A Thermodynamic Explanation of Symbolic Behavior" (1991, 22-26), provides useful criteria for determining the scale of a society by assessing monuments. This information does not give much evidence about the lives of the everyday people, but given that African history is improperly viewed as a history of many small disconnected ethnic groups, the interpretation of monuments would seem to be a valid method of obtaining primary source data on large-scale societies.

One of the first excavations in Nubia was conducted by G.A. Reisner in 1913 and 1916 and published in 1923 by the Peabody Museum of Harvard University: *Excavations at Kerma,* Part I-III & Part IV-V. He spent eighteen years excavating in Nubia. According to Shinnie (1982), Meroe became of major interest to archaeologists after A.H. Sayce (1912) reported that Meroe must have been the "Birmingham of Africa" and might have supplied the whole of Africa with iron implements (17-18). It is tempting to declare that Meroe was responsible for the dispersion of iron technology in Africa; however that might be overstating the case. Nevertheless, in their 1982 paper, "Meroitic Iron Working" Shinnie and Kense provide evidence that "the form of bowl bellows [in Meroe] ...suggests that they were operated much as those in subsequent African societies" (27). Moreover, the earliest forms of other iron-smelting furnaces in Africa—Taruga in Nigeria and Katruks in Tanzania—used similar bellows during the same period, the middle of the first millennium C.E. (27). I am primarily concerned here with cultural similarities among Kush and Kemet and the rest of Africa, and will not explore the diffusion of iron technology in Africa.

George Reisner is considered to be the founder of Meroitic studies. His volumes contain extensive archeological data and descriptions of an excavated cemetery containing thousands of graves, some containing over 322 human sacrifices. This evidence was interpreted as indicative of a highly centralized political authority at Kerma, and possibly state formation. Reisner interpreted this material evidence within a Eurocentric paradigm that viewed dominance and competition as the driving forces of society. He classified the people buried in Kerma as either (a) Nubianized Egyptians of the Middle Kingdom or (b) Kerma officials (known as the Viceroys of Kush). I do not deny historical evidence that Kemet at some point ruled parts of Nubia. Nevertheless, the people of Nubia had their own culture that was not just an imitation of Kemet. At times, upper Kemet and lower Nubia were united and kings from Kush ruled a united Kemet and Kush. The common cosmogonies, totems, kingship patterns and other evidence by provided by scholars (DuBois 1916, 1965, 1975; Williams 1989) indicate common origins. Reisner's *Excavations at Kerma [1923]* is still used today. I will assess the relevant archeological findings below.

Intellectual Heritage of Eurocentricism

The definition of what is an African is at the core of the issue of Eurocentric historiography concerning Kush and other parts of Africa. Those who stand against the interests of African people have sought to define the importance and place of African people and Africa in history and in current events. The thought-patterns of the fathers of Eurocentric history are with us still.

It is often said that the most quoted historian is Georg Wilhelm Friedrich Hegel (1770-1831), who was a professor of philosophy at the University of Berlin from 1818 until his death. Asante posits that Hegel's influence is so deep that the problem with the Eurocentric frame of reference concerning research method is that it is grounded in Hegel's conception of history (1990, 23). Hegel theorized that in order to understand a people's culture it was necessary to understand their history. He developed the theory of dialectics, later expanded upon by Karl Marx and others. Hegel in this theory determines what necessarily had to happen and what constitutes progress and the constituents of confrontational phases. Using these elements, Hegel wrote *The Philosophy of History* (1899) in which he attempts to survey the history of the world.

Since the focus of the present book is Africa, however, let us analyze some of Hegel's statements concerning Africa. He first divides the world into three parts—Africa, Asia, and Europe (91). He then divides Africa into three parts—Africa proper, European Africa, and the Nile Valley (91). These divisions continue to be used today. Of so-called Africa proper, Hegel declares:

> Africa proper, as far as History goes back, has remained—for all purposes of connection with the rest of the World—shut up, it is the Gold-land compressed within itself—*the land of childhood, which lying beyond the day of self-conscious history*, is enveloped in the dark mantle of Night...the interior...a girdle of marsh land with the most luxuriant vegetation, the especial home of ravenous beasts, snakes of all kinds—a border tract whose atmosphere is poisonous to Europeans...*[the Negro] hordes have exhibited the most reckless inhumanity and disgusting barbarism [towards themselves], [however] they showed themselves mild and well disposed towards the Europeans....*[emphasis added] (91-92)

This view of Africa as disconnected from the "world" is evident today in terms such as "sub-Saharan Africa;" in statements such as Paul S. Shinnie's (1982) regarding the misplaced hopes of developing a comprehensive and coherent history of Africa (17); and in Graham Connah's (1987) statement concerning the insurmountable Sahara desert and his need to continue the practice of beheading Africa (21). The use of words such as "childhood," "night," "hordes," "barbarism," "inhumanity," and "snakes" (a symbol of evil in European culture, but a symbol of resurrection in many African cultures) indicate Hegel's negative valorization of Africa. The negative image of Africans as being inhumane to each other but well-disposed toward Europeans is still evident today in news stories concerning the violence in Rwanda and Liberia and relief efforts of Europeans. Hegel next expounds on the Nile Valley:

> The second portion of Africa is the river district of the *Nile—Egypt: which was adapted to become a mighty centre of independent civilization, and therefore is as isolated and singular in Africa as Africa itself appears in relation to the other parts of the world* [emphasis added]. The northern part of Africa...was to be—*must* [emphasis original] be—attached to Europe. (92-93)

First Hegel divided Africa into parts, then he assigned values to the parts. Thus separating the Nile Valley from other parts of Africa and attaching it to Europe or Asia is a practice that continues to permeate Africology (Reisner 1923; Adams 1977; White 1970; Connah 1987; Robins 1993). Hegel proceeds by positing Africa as the ultimate Other:

> The peculiarly African character is difficult to comprehend, for the very reason that in reference to it, *we must quite give up the principle which naturally accompanies all our ideas—the category of Universality. In Negro life the characteristic point is the fact that consciousness has not yet attained to the realization of any substantial objective existence—as for example, God, or Law*—in which the interest of man's volition is involved and in which he realizes his own being...the Knowledge of an absolute being, an Other and a Higher than his individual Self, is entirely wanting...*there is nothing harmonious with humanity to be found in*

> *this type of character* [emphasis added].
> (1899, 93)

First of all, this is blatantly untrue. The worship of a Supreme Being by Africans permeates the culture. John Mbiti (1969) in his seminal work *African Religions and Philosophy* describes the importance of a Supreme Being in African culture:

> African knowledge of God is expressed in proverbs, short sentences, songs, prayers, names, myths, stories and religious ceremonies. All these are easy to remember and pass on to other people, since there are no sacred writings in traditional societies. *One should not, therefore, expect long dissertations about God. But God is no stranger to African peoples, and in traditional life there are no atheists* [emphasis added]....(29)

Hegel assumes that Africans do not worship a Supreme Being because he is unaware of—or more correctly, unable to comprehend—any African sacred texts or distinct modes of worship. Sacred texts are in the everyday language of the people and in many cultures such as the Nile Valley they *were* written; and places of worship are wherever the people are located.

This brings us to the second problem with Hegel's text. It is ethnocentric. The historiography of Africa is laden with value statements about Africa based solely on comparisons with Europe. Hegel expresses some positive value in so-called sub-Saharan Africa only where he sees Islam. "Mohammedanism," he declares, "appears to be the only thing which in any way brings the Negro within the range of culture" (93). This is because two "core-values" of Islam are writing and monotheism, which also are highly valued in the West. Preiswerk and Perrot (1978), in *Ethnocentrism and History,* define ethnocentrism as follows:

> ...the attitude of a group which consists of attributing to itself a central position compared to other groups, valuing positively its achievements and particular characteristics, adopting a projective type of behavior toward out-groups and interpreting the out-group though the in-group's mode of thinking....*In this sense, the notion of ethnocentrism is synonymous with that of cultural "centrism"* [emphasis added]. (14)

This Eurocentrism and ethnocentrism allows Hegel (1899) to place a high positive value on the enslavement of Africans because "*slavery is itself a phase of advance* from the merely isolated sensual existence—a phase of education—a *mode of becoming participant in a higher morality and the culture connected with it*" [emphasis added] (99). It is this same Eurocentrism and ethnocentric chauvinism which allows W. Y. Adams (1977) to write:

> Meroitic civilization is no more the simple and direct culmination of Napatan civilization than is Ptolemaic Egypt the climax of the pharaonic ages. Each represents a major cultural renaissance after centuries of stagnation and decline. *The revitalizing force in each case was the same: contact with, and partial integration into, the classical world* [emphasis added]. (295)

Again African cultures are valorized positively or negatively based on contact with or similarity to the West.

Thirdly, Hegel's use of the concept of "universality" is also problematic. It is a term that is widely accepted and utilized by Eurocentric scholars. Marimba Ani (1993) elucidates on the reason this term is problematic from an Afrocentric world-view:

> The projection of so-called "universalism" as assumed goal of human behavior is not

> desirable or culturally meaningful, but it allows European particularism as something other than it is. The claim to "universality" whether made by a Christian apologist, a social theorist, or a military leader is merely a packaging device....The real question becomes, Why has the European made so much of this claim of universalism? (193)

This packaging device becomes "the most subtle and ideologically effective manifestation of European cultural imperialism" (511). Thus Hegel denies Africans universality and membership in the human race because they do not worship a Supreme Being in the same manner as Europeans.

I contend that it is a similar abhorrence of African culture that underlies the effort of Eurocentric scholars to disassociate the Nile Valley from the rest of Africa. As W. Y. Adams (1977), the preeminent scholar on Nubia, has explicitly written: "I am...*resentful* of efforts to place [Nubians] in *a historical pigeonhole as 'Africans' or 'blacks'* [emphasis added](8). Conversely, it is unheard of for a scholar writing about ancient Gaul to be resentful of efforts to place it within European history or to call the diverse ethnic groups of France "white."

Because the supremacy of the Nile Valley civilizations cannot be denied, Hegel's only recourse, given his Eurocentric position on Africa, is to define them as non-African. He thus pronounces:

> At this point we leave Africa, not to mention it again. For it is no historical part of the World: it has no movement or development to exhibit. *Historical movements in it—this is in its northern part—belong to the Asiatic or European World* [emphasis added]. (99)

Arnold Toynbee was a professor of history at the University of London and the director of the Royal Institute of

International Affairs. He was proficient in Greek and Arabic and was married to the daughter of a highly respected professor of Hellenic studies. "Each year since 1926 he...published a volume setting forth the situations in various countries, including the most remote, which serves as a handbook of information in the international politics of England. In 1934 he published the first three volumes of his prodigious work *A Study Of History*, and in 1939 another three volumes" (Ortega Y Gasset 1973, 11). Toynbee was considered to be one the most preeminent scholars of universal history (11). In that position, as the above quote reveals, he was also a top advisor in international affairs. This network of academic and public affairs affects African historiography, archaeology, anthropology, and the position of Africa today in world politics.

In discussing the cause of the genesis of civilization, Toynbee (1934) assesses:

> ...the contributions which peoples of the several races of Man, as classified by color, have actually made to our twenty-one civilizations. We will confine our attention to active, creative contributions, leaving mere passive membership out of account (for, if we took account of that, we should have to inscribe, as contributors on the contemporary Western Civilization, the entire living generation of Mankind). (232)

He locates the "Egyptiac" peoples as belonging to the white "Alpine" and white "Mediterranean" races (232). In his footnotes explaining why he places them in two white races, Toynbee refers to the writings of craniologist Elliot Smith (whose work we have already addressed) and *The Cambridge Ancient History*, Volume I. Again we have a demonstration of Cheikh Anta Diop's dictum that "The birth of Egyptology was marked by the need to destroy the memory of a Negro Egypt at any cost and in all minds. Henceforth, the common denominator of all the theses of the Egyptologists, the close relationship and profound affinity, can be characterized as a desperate attempt to refute that opinion. Almost all Egyptologists stress its falsity as a matter of course" (1974, 45).

Toynbee narrows down his definition of civilization further by attributing to the Black race no contributions:

> It will be seen that, when we classify Mankind by color, the only one of the primary races, given by this classification which has not made a creative contribution to any of our twenty-one civilizations is the *Black Race* [emphasis original]. (233)

Toynbee does not place the race of the Nubians on this particular chart; however, he makes his position clear in other passages:

> The classic Southern March was only a march so long as *the First Cataract marked a sharp line of cultural division between the Egyptiac Civilization and a Nubian barbarism....The Egyptiac Civilization was... exotic in Nubia*; and such interaction between the two cultures as took place in that age resulted in the barbarization of the Egyptian garrison and not in the civilizing of the Nubian proletariat [emphasis added]. (114-115)

The race of the Nubians must be Black, in his opinion, for the sharp line of cultural division and the exotic placement of Egypt in Nubia seems to be because of the difference in races. These divisions were so great, in his view, that the Egyptians were debased by mere contact with the Nubians. The same notion in more modern dress appears in the statement of archeologist, J.E. Manchip White, when he explains that Piankhi (Piye)[2] withdrew after (what White views as) his conquest of Egypt because the Egyptians were white, and the "Negroes felt ill-at-ease among the fair-skinned Egyptians" (1970, 190). Again, we see the view that the cultural and racial demarcations between Nubia and Egypt were so great that the king who saved them felt so little self-worth that he could not live with his so-called superiors. I will demonstrate that this position is totally unfounded.

Eurocentric scholars (willy-nilly, it seems) either locate Nubia as part of the Nile Valley civilization, which they classify as a subdivision of Asia or of the Mediterranean; or as Negroid and African and therefore culturally different from Kemet. In either event peoples of African descent and their cultures are ranked as inferior to the peoples and cultures of Europe. Thomas Jefferson (1790) articulates this position well:

> I advance it, therefore, as a suspicion only, that the blacks, whether originally a distinct race or made distinct by time and circumstance, are inferior to the whites in the endowments of both body and mind. (Jordan 1968, 439)

Homage to the Elders

There were many elders upon whose shoulders a book such as this stands. They have laid the groundwork to establish the African character of Kush and Kemet and fought battles that are still being waged today. In the tradition of the people of the Nile Valley, they are ancestors to whom respect must be given for this book to be placed in its proper context.

W.E.B. DuBois sought to set the historical record straight. He was the first to attempt a comprehensive history of people of African descent. His efforts on the behalf of historical truth on Africa were: *The Negro* (1916); *Black Folk Then and Now* (1939), and *The World and Africa: An Inquiry Into The Part Which Africa Has Played In World History* (1946). DuBois attempts to extract Africa from the narrow margins of European history. He laments in *The Negro* (1916) that "there are those who would write universal history and leave out Africa" (5).

DuBois demonstrates what I refer to as nascent Afrocentricity. This is not the paradigm shift that was later to be developed by Molefi Asante (1990) in which he emphatically states that "no longer can European studies of Africa parade as African studies: the overthrow of the dominating canon has already begun" (7). However, DuBois does locate African history as essential to the understanding of humans. "I am seeking in this book [*The World and Africa*] to remind readers...of how critical a part Africa has played in human history, past and present, and how impossible it is to forget this and rightly explain the present plight of mankind" (vii). Clearly in his nascent Afrocentric analysis DuBois is aware that where one stands is at the heart of the epistemological issue. "At any rate," he declares, "here is a history of the world written from the African point of view, or better, a history of the Negro as part of the world which now lies in ruins" (viii).

DuBois' historical writings are beneficial to the present work because of his placement of African history at the center of human history. Moreover, DuBois believed that the treatment of the Nile Valley in archeology, anthropology, and history is a good indicator of a racist foundation. The enslavement of Africans and the capitalist empire built on the backs of these enslaved Africans affected knowledge and intellectual honesty. One of the tools used to justify the enslavement of African people was the sophistic manipulation of the records of the Nile Valley cultures. The excellence of the Nile Valley had to be placed outside of the scope of African people. DuBois reinstates ancient Egypt and the rest of the Nile Valley in Africa. "Of what race, then, were the Egyptians? They were certainly not white in any sense of the modern word..." (17).

He continues by connecting Kemet culturally with the rest of Africa, a concept that is also key to the present work. This is a concept that was later developed by Diop (1974) and Theophile Obenga (1974) and others. DuBois demonstrated tremendous foresight in postulating this connection in *The Negro* (1916), his first work on African history. "The evidence of language also connects Egypt with Africa and the Negro race rather than with Asia, while religious ceremonies and social customs all go to strengthen this evidence" (19).

Indeed DuBois had to deal with the attempt to steal Egypt away from Africa. DuBois addresses the crux of the issue in *The World and Africa* (1946) and proceeds to reconstruct history based on the truth. DuBois pronounces that:

> [A]lmost unanimously in the nineteenth century Egypt was not regarded as part of Africa....It is especially significant that the science of Egyptology arose and flourished at the very time that the cotton kingdom reached its greatest power on the foundation of American Negro slavery....*We may then without further ado ignore this verdict of history...and treat Egyptian history as an integral part of African history* [emphasis added]. (99)

DuBois exhibits in this passage the power of owning knowledge. As Afrocentric psychologist Wade Nobles (1985) declares, "Power is the ability to define reality and have other people respond to your definition as if it were their own" (107). This present work will treat the history of the people of the Nile Valley as an integral part of African history and as part of the reality of African people.

William Leo Hansberry, another elder in the reclaiming of Nile Valley history, provides us with a measure of the impact of DuBois' work. Hansberry recounts that after reading *The Negro* (1916), "Dr. DuBois' references to and notices of cultures, kingdoms, and empires in other parts of Black Africa amounted to a revelation which, despite all previous reading, took me completely by surprise" (Clark 1970, 101). Hansberry's "discovery" of that made this book a turning point in his life. In a curvilinear role-exchange, by the time DuBois wrote *The World and Africa* (1946), *he* credits *Hansberry* with providing him most of his material on Ethiopia, which included Nubia. Among Hansberry's many works, two specifically relate to the Nile Valley: *Sources for the Study of Ethiopian History* (1977) and *Pillars in Ethiopian History* (1947).

David Walker, in his *Appeal to the Coloured Citizens of the World but in Particular and Very Expressly to Those of the United States of America* (1829), examined the Kemites because, so frequently (continuing to this day), references were made comparing their slave system to America's. He stated "Egyptians were Africans...such as we are—some of them yellow and others dark—a mixture of Ethiopians and natives of Egypt—about the same as you see the coloured people of the United States at the present day" (9).

African people have long been involved in the struggle for the liberation of information about the Nile Valley from its Eurocentric hegemonic hold. Hosea Easton in 1837 published *A Treatise On The Intellectual Character of the Colored People of the United States* in which he asserts that the Egyptians transmitted their knowledge to the Greeks (Association For the Study of Classical African Civilization, *Africa: Dispelling The Myths* [1992], c-1). Edward Wilmot Blyden visited Egypt and entered the pyramid of Khufu. He published "The Negro In Ancient History" in 1869 in the *Methodist Quarterly Review*. He compiled information from the Bible and from contemporary authors such as Count Volney, regarding the African foundation of Ancient Egyptian civilization (c-1). Martin Delaney in 1879 published *Principles of Ethnology: Origins of Races and Color with An Archaeological Compendium of Ethiopian And Egyptian Civilization* (c-2). Rufus L. Perry published *The Cushites, Or The Children of Ham As Seen By the Ancient Historians and Poets* in 1887 (c-2) which also characterizes the Kemites as Africans. Frederick Douglass travelled to Kemet in 1886, three decades after having discussed the blackness of the Ancient Egyptian in a speech in Rochester, N.Y. (1854) entitled "The Claim of the Negro Ethnologically Considered: An Address" (c-2). Following a trip to Cairo in 1887, he wrote in a letter to his son:

> It has been the fashion of American writers, to deny that the Egyptians were Negroes and claim that they are the same race of themselves. This has, I have no doubt, been largely due to a wish to deprive the Negro of the moral support of Ancient Greatness and to appropriate the same to the white race. (McFeely 1991, 331-332)

Staking a claim for African Americans, Alain Leroy Locke was present in Ipet Isut (Luxor), Kemet, at the reopening of the tomb of King Tutankhamen. He was representing Howard University and the Negro Society for Historical Research (ASCAC, c-2).

Drusilla Dunjee Houston in 1926 published *Wonderful Ethiopians of the Ancient Cushite Empire, Book I*. This is one of the only books written by a person of African ancestry that is dedicated to Kush. Ms. Houston did a remarkable job, given the resources available to her. Her position on the Nile Valley civilization was that the most ancient world civilization unfolded in the Nile Valley through the efforts of African people and, secondly, that from this most ancient African civilization others were developed, such as Arabian, Babylonian, Indian, Hindu, and Ancient Median and Persian.

Afrocentric educator Asa G. Houston, III comments on the significance of Drusilla D. Houston's scholarship in the afterword of his recent book:

> Drusilla Dunjee Houston avoided a major conceptual problem by her choice of a title for her book. It was a master stroke for her to focus on the Cushite Empire with reference to the fact that they were "Ethiopians." To have done it the other way around, i.e., to have focused on Ethiopia alone, would have been a mistake of major proportions. For it was the work of the Blacks or "Ethiops" in nation building that is of prime interest....Houston's focus is upon African

> *peoplehood* [emphasis original] rather than upon Black individuals.... *What is missing in African history presentations is the basic story of a people* [emphasis added]...(1985, i-ii)

Houston's thesis on the Kushite origins of various peoples has been substantiated by more recent findings (Diop 1974; Pimienta-Bey 1993; Van Sertima 1976).

Yosef Ben-Jochannan, a forerunner in Kemetology, visited Kemet for the first time in 1939. He has provided copious evidence of the African foundations of Kemet and Kush in many works such as *Africa: Mother of Western Civilization* (1971) and *Black Man of the Nile and His Family* (1981). He declares:

> If there is a country and people in history that should receive the MOST MALIGNED award it is Nubia and the Nubians—the so-called "Negroes." Why? Egypt and Nubia, as Merowe, and sometimes Kush, shared identical writing, culture, Gods, agriculture, science, medicine: and at varied times they also shared common HEAD-OF-STATE called "PHARAOH" (King) [emphasis original]. (1971, 292)

St. Clair Drake's *Black Folk Here and There* (1987), using the tools of anthropology, proceeds through copious research, diagrams, maps, and high quality photographs to provide a tour-de-force of historiography on Nile Valley civilizations, and the role of Black people in those civilizations. The breadth of his scholarship ranges from predynastic times to the Hellenic influence. He extracts bountiful information from racist scholars, such as Arthur Weigall, who has a chapter in *Personalities of Antiquity* (1932) entitled "The Exploits of a Nigger King"; from 'old scrappers' such as Chancellor Williams; and from European classicists, such as Frank Snowden. Snowden provides a model for scholarship *par excellence* with his clear thinking and judicious use of a wide range of material. He seeks not merely to provide information, but also to pique the interest of scholars to explore topics and expand upon his research. Indeed, he does accomplish these goals.

Drake, however, remains tied to the discipline of anthropology, and this restricts his vision. Thus, he uses terms (such as "Near East") that essentially serve the interests of the Europeans, and he labels some African ethnic groups as marginal peoples. Furthermore, because he still has an interest in his discipline, he does not take a firm stand in the interests of African people on key points. Drake, writing in 1988, could have strengthened his work by incorporating the Afrocentric paradigm.

Drake attempts to show in this volume that discrimination on the basis of color is a mere factor of historical need, and Ancient Nile Valley civilizations are excellent examples of the absence of this discrimination prior to the European enslavement of African people.

Cheikh Anta Diop's work is the foundation upon which the present work is built. He challenged Africa-centered scholars, by writing:

> The African historian who evades the problem of Egypt is neither modest nor objective, nor unruffled, he is ignorant, cowardly and neurotic. Imagine, if you can the unfortunate position of a Western historian who was to write the history of Europe without referring to Greco-Latin antiquity and try to pass that off as a scientific approach. (1974, xiv)

I will seek to meet Diop's criterion and extend the concept of Ancient Kemet to include the civilization of Nubia, particularly the era of Kush, and to use the Nile Valley as the African Classical civilization.

Diop in his last book, *Civilization Or Barbarism* (1981), posits the cultural unity of Kemet and Kush, based on the assumed cultural commonalities of Africa and on evidence provided by archeologist Bruce Williams.

Williams' article in *Archeology* (1980, 12-21), reprinted in Ivan Van Sertima's "The Lost Pharaohs of Nubia" in *Egypt Revisited* (1980, 90-104), brought to the public's attention a stone incense burner found during excavations conducted by the University of Chicago during the UNESCO's International Salvage Campaign of 1963-64. [The complete results of the archeological investigations were reported and summarized in, *Oriental Institute Nubian Expedition, Vol. V.; Excavations between Abu Simbel and the Sudan Frontier, Part 5: C-Group, Pan Grave and Kerma Remains At Adindan Cemeteries T, K, U and J.*] This burner depicts a king in a royal boat, wearing the white crown of Kemet, a palace *serekh*, and a representation of the falcon god, Heru. This is the most ancient depiction of a king in the Nile Valley or anywhere else in history. Diop does not mention that Williams' team also found several other incense burners "depicting a combination of ships and palace facades in royal procession" (18) and other Predynastic art reflecting an unnamed feline deity, a man saluting, and two animals (an antelope and a carnivore) frolicking next to a ship. These artifacts were all found in one of the richest and earliest tombs in Cemetery 1 in Ancient Nubia. Through the context in which they were found, the quality and quantity of the wealth of the cemetery, and the style and composition of the incense burners, the date of these items was determined to be about six or seven generations before the dynastic era in Kemet (13-21).

Diop states that based on this evidence we can better understand "the matriarchal essence of Egyptian royalty and the importance of the role of the queen-mother in Nubia, Egypt, and the rest of Black Africa" ([1955] 1974, 105); divine kingship; and why the Kemetic word for royalty (*nsw* in hieroglyphics) meant the man "who came from the South." It also helps to clarify why the people of Kemet always "turned toward the South," just as Moslems turn toward Mecca. This present work establishes that during the period when Kemet was ruled by foreigners from the North during the 25th Dynasty, the people turned to the South once again, and Piye (Piankhi) answered their call.

Diop traces the crux of the Eurocentric analysis of Ancient Kemet and Kush to the very beginnings of the discipline of Egyptology. In *The African Origin of Civilization: Myth or Reality* ([1955] 1974), Diop posits that because of imperialism and the *maafa* of enslavement, Egyptologists stress the concept that the ancient Egyptians were not black.

Summary

The indisputable position of African people in world history must be elucidated. Kushites have not been viewed from a holistic African perspective. Kushite history has become obfuscated by the discourse concerning the place of the Nile Valley in African history. Eurocentric scholars have been incapable of writing a holistic history of the Kushites because they have negatively valorized all Africans outside of ancient Egypt. These scholars continue to disassociate cultural characteristics of Nile Valley cultures from those found in what they have termed "Africa south of the Sahara."

The perspective of this book is different because it is written with the tools of the Afrocentric perspective. The foundation of this book is the assumption that African peoplehood can be analyzed through a set of common cultural attributes. These cultural commonalities have been explicated by Cheikh Anta Diop in *The African Origin of Civilization* ([1955] 1974) and further elaborated upon in *Civilization or Barbarism* (1991). Thus, Diop has given us a set of criteria through which one can analyze African cultures. Our research has not uncovered any other book which has taken an Afrocentric approach to Kushite culture.

NOTES

1. This is from a song entitled *War*. Bob Marley writes that this was a speech "by H.I.M. Haile Selassie I King of Kings, Lord of Lords, the Conquering Lion of the tribe of Judah. California 28th February 1968."

2. It is now common practice to write this king's name as Piye. The *ankh* is believed to be used only as a symbol of life. However, the present writer prefers to use Piankhi, on the grounds that the presence of the *ankh* in his name apparently had some spiritual significance to the Kushite king.

CHAPTER THREE

EMANCIPATING THE STUDY OF AFRICAN CULTURE AND HISTORY

Eurocentric historiography concerning Kush still rests on racist and ethnocentric underpinnings. Kemetologist Wade Nobles, trained as an experimental social psychologist and the most quoted author of Afrocentric psychology, observes that this is a common problem:

> The whole field of Egyptology and the treatment of African contributions to human civilization can be understood as partly the transubstantive errors of investigators who gave erroneous meaning to "things" African ...*knowing is rigidly controlled by the methodology or mechanism of destruction, distortion, fabrication, suppression and confusion"* [emphasis added]. (1986, 19-20)

The Afrocentric methodology of analyzing words, concepts, and all information from the perspective of the interests of African people enabled the author of the present work to overcome "scientific colonialism."

Molefi Asante, the originator of the discipline of Afrocentricity, the editor of *The Journal of Black Studies,* and the Chair of Temple University's Department of African-American Studies, has written a series of books on Afrocentric theory. He lays out the parameters of the discipline of Afrocentricity in *Kemet, Afrocentricity and Knowledge* (1990). The protest against European domination of knowledge did not originate with Asante, but other theorists who have denounced the Europe-centered perspective have "hedged their bets" (vi) because they still have a vested interest in the maintenance of the system. The Afrocentric method does not seek to maintain a system that has historically demonstrated that it is not operating in the interests of African people. Asante forthrightly declares this when he writes that he seeks "to overthrow parochialism, provincialism, and narrow Wotanic visions of the world by demonstrating the usefulness of an Afrocentric approach to questions of knowledge" (1990, vi). It is in this spirit that I employ the Afrocentric method.

Asante explains that the "Afrocentric enterprise is framed by cosmological, epistemological, axiological, and aesthetic issues. In this regard the Afrocentric method pursues a world voice distinctly African-centered...How do we gather meaning out of African or other existence?" (1990, 8). This research is primarily an epistemological issue. I seek to find meaning out of the culture of Kush using criteria delineated by Cheikh Anta Diop related to commonalities of African cultures. I seek, in the use of the Afrocentric method, to know the Kushite culture as part of a holistic picture of African peoplehood. It thus also involves axiological issues. Cultural commonalities among African cultures is assumed to be good and informs the method of knowing. Asante proclaims that "Our methodology must be holistic and integrative; our epistemology, participatory and committed. The Africologist is a working scholar committed to the advancement of knowledge about

the African world" (28). Knowledge of African people is advanced through the use of the Afrocentric methodology.
The orientation of Africans to the cosmos is different from that of people of European descent. Hence, cosmological issues concerning the place of spirituality in the culture of Kush also are addressed. The issue of the role of spirit is essential to any Afrocentric analysis. John Mbiti (1969), Professor of Religious Studies at Makere University, Uganda, and Director of the Ecumenical Institute, Bossey, Switzerland, declares:

> The physical and spiritual are but two dimensions of one and the same universe. These dimensions dove-tail into each other to the extent that at times and in places one is apparently more real than, but not exclusive of, the other. To African peoples this religious universe is not an academic proposition: it is an empirical experience, which reaches its height in acts of worship. (Mbiti [1969] 1990, 57)

I will examine the Kushite culture for evidence that the people of Kush viewed the world from a similar perspective.

Using an Afrocentric methodology will involve delinking and re-confirming. Asante postulates that re-confirmation means "the scholar pursues the organic, Diopian unity of African thought, symbols, and ritual concepts to their classical origins" (56). This is the objective of this analysis. De-linking entails removing the African people from the margins of history. This study seeks to remove Africa from the perimeters of Kushite history and position it in the nucleus of the analysis.

This location of African culture at the center will assist in understanding the deep structure of Kushite culture. C.T. Keto, an historian and South African activist, postulates in the only book written specifically about Afrocentric historiography, *The Africa Centered Perspective of History* (1989), that historians must "openly specify the particular regional 'center' on the globe which provides the fulcrum upon which they anchor historical events and, therefore human meaning and interpretation" (2). The meaning of many components of Kushite culture has been unclear to many scholars in the past, because they did not anchor Kush in Africa. This method will give new meaning to Kushite culture.

In fact, an Afrocentric methodology requires a wholesale rewriting of history. African history had been in the bondage of European supremacy. The freedom which comes from viewing the same information with eyes focused on the interests of Africa will invariably reveal new insights. Cheikh Anta Diop expected that with the underpinning of a classical culture—ancient Egypt—Afrocentric historiography would be transformed. He explains that Afrocentric historiography makes it necessary to rewrite world history from a more scientific standpoint, taking into account the Negro-African component which was for a long time preponderant. It means that it is now possible to build up a corpus of Negro-African humanities resting on a sound historical basis instead of being suspended in mid-air....The cause of human progress is not well served by casting a veil over the facts. (1981, 50-51)

Aesthetics will also be addressed. Much of what we know about Kushite culture has been interpreted through a reading of the carvings on tombs and other objects, such as libation tables. We will seek to comprehend the aesthetic practices of the Kushite people from an African centered position. The art of Kush is magnificent and absorbing. However, like all African art, it is meant to be understood on various levels. It is not mere ornamentation; it is symbolic and rich in meaning. The jewelry is also symbolic and meant to be understood on a spiritual level.

Professor Kariamu Welsh Asante, Director of the International Institute for African Dance and Research in the Department of African American Studies at Temple University, has written about African aesthetics from a holistic perspective. In *African Culture: Rhythms of Unity* (1990), she postulates that "An historical, mythological, and religious world-view must be undertaken to understand the African aesthetic" (73). The historical perspective which will place Kush firmly in Africa allows us to better understand its "art." Unlike the European aesthetic, "[t]he signature of the African artist is inherent in the creation and the spiritual or divine creator deserves and is given the credit. It is understood that the artist is a conduit and therefore not responsible for the greatness of the work" (73). These are the principles from which Kushite aesthetic values will be viewed.

I do not claim objectivity. Previous studies on Kush have been conducted with a hidden agenda. I have sought to operate in the interests of African people. This does not negate a scholarly approach. The combination of thought and feeling applied to Afrocentric methodology adds a dimension to the study of Kush that is lacking in research which seeks to understand it with thought only.

The soul of Afrocentric methodology situates the energies of the Kushite culture within the rhythms of Africa. For example, many researchers are still in a quandary as to the reason the Kemites welcomed the 25th dynasty as victors returning home and not conquerors. The reason is simply that Piankhi (Piye) began the process of restoring Maát and reached back to the Old Kingdom to revitalize the culture.

An Afrocentric methodology frees the researcher to seek the spiritual meaning in addition to the material one. Molefi Asante describes how this can be achieved:

> Soul is the vitality the researcher brings to the Afrocentric method, that is, the creative energy used to effect a successful project. The concept is similar to Wade Nobles' idea of cultural substance which he sees as the "ontological principle of consubstantiation." But I mean something more than the ontological principle when I say soul of method. This is not a mere oxymoron but what the Yoruba often call the Ase,' the force itself....The indwelling vital energy must be present in the scholar's work for it to be

successful....Indeed, the human personality keeps Ase' active and vital. In research, the scholar must understand that everything is potentially active, powerful, and possible and it is up to the scholar to access the vitality of a project. (1990, 107-108)

I will proceed from the premise that material and spiritual matters in the culture were vital forces. This distinguishes the present work from other books written about Kush.

CHAPTER FOUR

AFRICAN CULTURAL COMMONALITIES

There are many cultural similarities among African people. In this chapter, we will survey research concerning similarities of cultural practices in Africa. This will provide us with a framework for our inquiry. Furthermore, it will demonstrate that the search for cultural parallels between Kemet and the rest of Africa has not been exclusively an Afrocentric undertaking.

Petrie's "Egypt in Africa"

Let us begin by examining a statement made by the famous Egyptologist, Flinders Petrie. In 1914, he published in the journal *Ancient Egypt*, of which he was editor, an article entitled "Egypt In Africa." He began by commenting on the gap that had been placed between Egypt and the rest of Africa:

> *Though as a matter of mere geography the continental position of Egypt had always been obvious, yet as a matter of humanity it has always appeared to be aloof from the*

> *rest of the continent, in a way that perhaps no other country is detached from its natural connection.* Egypt has always stood at a far higher level of civilization than any other part of Africa, for the links with Syria, Crete, or Greece have been leading factors. So far have these connections prevailed that *we need now to recall with care how largely the earliest stratum of Egyptian ideas has been at one with the rest of Africa* [emphasis added]. (115)

It is interesting that Petrie noted that no other civilization has been perceived as being so separate from "its natural connection." That Petrie is here speaking from an Eurocentric perspective is evident from his linear method of placing Egypt at a higher level of civilization than the rest of Africa; and from his implication that the ancient Egyptians felt more connected to Greece than Africa.[1] Nonetheless, in this article he provides us with useful information concerning the similarities of Kemet, the classical civilization, and the rest of Africa.

He attributes the various cultural similarities to three possible factors: (1) parallel development of thought without any physical connection; (2) direct descent from a common source; (3) the direct borrowing of details which only belong to the Old Kingdom and earlier, and which disappeared before the Nubian conquests of Egypt began (115). He discredits the first and third factors and focuses on similarities that are due to direct descent from a common source.

Petrie found sixty similarities, but eliminates four or five of them as being due to Greco-Roman influences. He found no evidence for ten of them, which left forty-five. Petrie declares that "As large a proportion as thirteen in forty-five is enough to show that direct descent is in general more likely than parallel development...such common source being in nearly all cases a primitive stock of population, and only rarely a later influence which passed through Egypt on its way into Africa." (116)

The evidence that he uses is from various scholars who had observed and interviewed various African ethnic groups, such as the Nyakang, Dinka, Babenda, Yaos, Galla, Akikuyu, Ankole, Unyoro, Nagadeh, Yaos, Ibo, New Calabar, Aro, and the Inoku. Petrie states that "Whether there be a direct borrowing of Egypt, a common descent, or even parallel development, such living view of the case before us must be an invaluable guide to understanding the proceeding and ideas of the ancient ceremonies and beliefs which were similar to those of modern times" (116).

Petrie divides the similarities between Kemet and the rest of Africa into two categories:

I. Treatment of the Body
1. Mummifying
2. Contracted burial
3. Beheading the dead
4. Passage for the spirit
5. Vehicle for the spirit
6. Restoration of ability to the corpse
7. Recess graves
8. Pole over grave
9. Round-domed graves
10. Domed pit tomb
11. Sloping tomb

II. Offerings for the Dead
12. Beer and flour offerings
13. Cloth offering
14. Offerings at the grave
15. Killing the offerings
16. Offering chamber above grave
17. Drain to the east
18. Men sacrificed at royal funeral
19. Eldest son the priest
20. The funeral image
21. Tall hats of officiants
22. Offering chamber for the image
23. The soul house

Petrie relates examples of various ethnic groups in "modern" Africa who observe the above cultural practices. The advantage of studying cultural practices in modern day groups is that one can ask questions of living practitioners and so gain a deeper level of understanding. Africans who were still participating in these practices at the time were living examples of culture similarities.

This article was part one of two parts. The second part, also called "Egypt in Africa," was completed by G.W.B. Huntingford in 1925 in the same journal, *Ancient Egypt*. He resumed Petrie's work by providing more evidence of connections in East Africa, particularly Kenya and Uganda. From a variety of sources and his own observations, Huntingford reports the following "institutions" as cultural similarities in Africa:

1. The chief as priest
2. Mundane spirit world
3. Every object has its spirit
4. Sacred fig-trees
5. Contracted burial
6. "The hyena"

Linguistic Connections

Huntingford traced linguistic similarities among the Nandi, the Masai, and the ancient Egyptians. Using the myth of the Hamites, he positions the Gala people as descendants of the people of Punt. He argues that the people of Punt are the common ancestors of the Hamites and the Egyptians. The Hamitic people, he conjectures, produced the Nandi and the Masai. What is advantageous to this analysis is that he assembled a list of eighteen words from the Kemetic and Nandi languages that have very striking resemblances. The list includes words that are essential to the culture, such as love, eat, sky, be ill, hand, and nose. Words such as these are so indispensable to a culture that they are typically not borrowed from another culture.

Parallels in African Religions

In 1922, Egyptologist N.W. Thomas published an article entitled "Dualism in African Religions" in the journal *Ancient Egypt*. Thomas investigates "the area of the Lower Niger, a centre of the reincarnation creed, which [he, Thomas]...brought into relation with the Egyptian belief of the *ka*" (109). The *ka* was the Kemetic symbol for the soul. Richard Wilkinson, who writes extensively on the interpretation of symbolism in Kemet, states that the *ka* was "used as a term for the creative and sustaining power of life. The *ka* was thus an aspect of the human being which came into being when the individual was born, and many representations show the ram-headed god Khnum fashioning the *ka* on his potters's wheel—as a double or twin of the individual child" (1994, 49). Thomas found a similar belief among other African people. He wrote that "The Edo of Benin City believe that each man had two *ehi* (geniuses or doubles, one good, the other bad); and precisely the same belief is found among the Ewe of Togoland, intimately related in language to the Edo" (109). He attributes the similarities in the belief in the *ka* to a diffusion of the culture of the so-called Hamitic tribes.

Thompson found only an "attenuated dualism" among so-called Negro tribes (Yoruba and Ibo) because to him "dualism is foreign to the negro mind" (110). This is not correct, of course, for the concept of duality or twinness permeates the African culture. For example, the Akan are, from all accounts known to this researcher, defined as "Negro." Their culture gives us an excellent example of the similarities of the use of the cultural concept of the *ka* in Kemetic and the *kra* in West African culture. In 1951, Eva L. R. Meyerowitz studied the "Concepts of the Soul Among The Akan of The Gold Coast." Writing in the journal *Africa*, she found that:

> When the bi-sexual deity of the cosmos Nyame Amowia, visible as the moon gave birth to the Sun god, she gave him her <u>kra</u>, *her eternal soul or life-giving power*; hence

his name, the Only Great Nyame (*Nyame*; *ko* - only; *pon* - great) generally drawn together as Nyankopon. The kra is also envisaged as bi-sexual; its female aspect is believed to be the substance or body of the moon and sun, i.e., fire, while its male aspect is the spirit, the essence, the spiritual or that which is truly divine [emphasis added]. (24)

In Kemetic culture we see a similar meaning of the *ka* symbol as a life force such as the *kra* functions as a life force. Concerning the *ka*, Richard Wilkinson informs us that:

> In coronation scenes...*the [ka]* is often formed by the overlapping arms of the deity who invests the king—thus providing *the symbolic giving of "life-power"* as well as the crown itself. This use is seen in the investiture of Hatshepsut depicted on her obelisk at Karnak and in the nearly identical coronation relief from the fallen obelisk of Thutmose III at the same location [emphasis added]. (1994, 49)

Another significant similarity is the treatment of the ka and its ability to live past the person. In Kemet:

> To "go to one's *ka*" meant "to die," however, as the *ka* continued to live on after the body died; and the priests served in the funerary cult were called *hemu—ka* or "Ka servants...." [I]t is possible that some of the subsidiary pyramids built during the Old Kingdom served this same purpose on a much larger scale. *Importantly, the ka needed continuing nourishment in order to survive and offering of food and drink were made to it.* Eventually, the offerings them-

> selves began to be regarded as being imbued with the *ka's* life-power, and the plural *kau* was used to mean "food-offerings" [emphasis added]. (*ibid.*)

The Akan held similar beliefs about the *kra*, as evidenced by the following practices:

> To become and remain immortal, all the various soul components, the *kra, honhon and saman* have to be again united, and this is achieved for the king and queen-mother in the rituals at the shrines for their souls...a chapel is erected...where the stools used in life by the deceased rulers are kept. *There the blackened stools act as shrines for the various parts of the souls of the departed and there the royal <u>kras</u> are fed on specified days. As long as food offerings are made to their <u>kras</u>, and their names uttered, the royal dead may live.* Should their kras not be fed, and shrines for the kra, the honhom (which is needed to supply the kra with the breath of life) and the saman no longer be maintained, the *kra* would become nameless and lose its personality. For the *kra* is the divine, impersonal component of the soul...[emphasis added]. (Meyerowitz 1951, 27)

When one has a holistic understanding of African culture, then the importance of spirituality in African culture becomes clear and indisputable (Ani 1993). It is not surprising then to see similarities in the practice of spirituality between the classical African culture (i.e., ancient Egypt) and those that followed it.

Seligman's "Egyptian Influence in Negro Africa"

C.G. Seligman (1934) inquired into "Egyptian Influence in Negro Africa" in *Studies Presented to F.LL. Griffith*. He was furthering research that he had begun sixteen years before at a Liverpool meeting of the British Association on "probable contacts between Egyptians and Negroes" (457). He ascribes the dispersion of common practices and customs to the Kemites and to those ancient folk whom I have named "the mythical Hamites." These are the common practices and customs that he found:

> The resemblance between throwing sticks[2] of Ancient Egypt and those of the Ingassa and other tribes of the hills of the Fung Province of the Anglo-Egyptian Sudan between the White and Blue Niles, is so obvious that even the laity see it and cast about for an explanation, which they immediately supply in terms of transmission due to contact. (457)

> The spiked wheel-trap, which is represented in the earliest known painted tomb of Egypt was recently found among the Ababdeh of the Eastern Desert...and in constant use among the tribes of the Upper Nile to the north of Lake Victoria, the Lango, Acholi, and others, as well as farther north among the Nuer. (457)

> In Uganda every king and king's son in addition to his clan totem claims the eagle as his totem, though no eagle exists, seems to point back to Egypt, where...in Hellenistic times eagle and falcon were confused. (457)

The anthropoid coffins of the Wagata, a tribe of the Belgian Congo...Coffin burial is sufficiently rare in Central Africa to be notable in itself, but when the coffins are such remarkable anthropoid structures as those represented on Pl. 73 there can...be very little doubt of their foreign, i.e., Egyptian origin." (458)

The idea of mummification...being considered so important that...the men of such tribes of the Lower Congo as the Bakongo, Basindi, and southern Bateke, save up all their lives in order to have a suitable supply [wrapping cloth] ready at their death. (458)

The *nametere*, used by the Lutuko people of the Sudan, "consists of a core of dry grass round which are wrapped a number of bamboos, to form a more or less cylindrical bundle representing the dead man....The *nametere* may be compared with the outward appearance of a poor Egyptian burial...it seems more probable that some experience or tradition of mummification, with poor success in preserving the body, had reached Black Africa and given rise to the Lotuko *nametere.*" (459-460)

The Dinka, Nuer and the Suk place high value on artificially deformed oxen horns. "Horns deformed in the style of the present-day Dinka and Nuer are represented in Egypt so long ago as the Vth Dynasty...can only signify that this is an Egyptian custom which spread up the Nile to Negro Africa." (460)

Jeffreys' "Diffusion of Cowries and Egyptian Culture in Africa"

Cowries were a system of currency found among various ethnic groups, including the Yoruba, Sobo, Igbo and Hausa. Cowries belong to a species of shells called mollusks, which also includes clams, conches, oysters, and snails. Cowries, like conches and snails, are univalves, meaning that they (unlike clams and oysters) have one shell. The tiger cowrie is found in the Indian and South West Pacific Oceans (*World Book Encyclopedia* 1985, 310-312). It is a salt-water shell, *but not indigenous to the Atlantic Ocean.*

There are two varieties of cowrie. One type, called the *mdudambu* by the Ibo, was no longer used as currency at the time of Jeffreys' writing (1948, 46). The other variety, called the *ayolo* by the Ibo, was used extensively as currency throughout Nigeria at the time of Jeffreys' writing. The technical name was *cyprea moneta* and it was found only in the Red Sea and the Indian Ocean (46). It was "distributed along the sea coast and along the main waterways of the Niger" (46). The use of these shells antedated the arrival of the Europeans. Jeffreys cites numerous European travellers who observed the use of cowries as currency when they first encountered West Africans. Also, Ibn Batuta mentions that he observed cowries being used as a medium of exchange in 1352. For example, Jeffreys quotes Gibb (1929), who wrote that:

> The existence of a cowry exchange in the Malli Empire alongside a salt exchange is conclusive of the commercial relations across the African continent...as cowries are found in Africa only on the east coast between the equator and Mozambique (Grand Encyclopedia S.V. Cauri). In Ibn Battuta's time, however, cowries were imported by merchants from the north. (47)

The parallels between the West African cowry enumeration system and that of ancient Kemet are remarkable. For example, Jeffreys observes "the Ibo, when counting mice and men, pots and pans, and so forth, use a decimal notation such as we use. But when counting cowries a notation based on a duodecimal system was used" (48).

> In these tribes the cowry has a system of enumeration different from that for enumeration in general. Can these systems based on six and sixty, like that of the English, be linked to Babylonia?...It seems far fetched where Africa, and especially West Africa, is concerned. A much more nearer source, Egypt, is available...When goods were weighed in ancient Egypt a system based on sixes was used. (50)

Trade would seem the most natural and commonsense explanation for such similarities in the use of a numeration system. If this had occurred in any other place but Africa, such an explanation would have been readily accepted. The similarities of many cultural practices among African peoples can also be explained through trade relations and common origins. Jeffreys proceeds:

> There is historical evidence to show commercial contacts across Africa. *The cowry shell in use comes from the East coasts of Africa and so fits in with the historical evidence.* In many tribes where the cowry is used as a monetary system a special form of notation is employed, and in many instances this notation is based on a unit involving six, either as a duodecimal or a sexagesimal notation. This type of notation is also found in ancient Egypt, which traded on the East coast of Africa as well as across Africa... Egypt...and the East coast of the Red Sea

and of Africa, are accessible from Ibo land by foot...(52)

Jeffreys also notes other resemblances between ancient Egypt and other African cultures, "namely: the Divine Kingship, the Dual Organization in Africa, the Winged Solar Disc, as well as the cowry, and many other resemblances found among the Ibo" (52).

H. Frankfort on "Modern Survivors From Punt"

Punt has a special role in Kemetic history. Most scholars concur that it was located in or around modern-day Somalia. Queen Hatshepsut's words and pictures on the walls of her temple Zeser Zeserou, "the Sublime of the Sublime," substantiate the importance of "divine land." She expressed intense pleasure when she received goods from Punt, especially incense trees for Amun (Erman 1894, 512). The following lines of a poem from ancient Egypt also demonstrate the significance of Punt to the Kemites:

> When I hold my love close
> (and her arms steal around me),
> *I'm like a man translated to Punt*
> or like someone out in the reedflats.
> (Foster 1974, 25)

H. Frankfort (1932) compares elements of the Puntite culture and that of Kemet. He postulates that "We know from the figures of Puntites in the New Kingdom...that the Egyptian did not distinguish them from himself in appearance; but under the Old Kingdom the same applies to the Nubians" (446). This is not to say that Frankfort believed that the ancient Egyptians, Puntites, or the Masai were Black or so-called Negro. Again, he, like others, used the Hamitic myth to distinguish "real negroes from fake negroes." He believes that Kemet "starts her career as a cultural power by differentiating herself from a definitely African civilization" (451). Frankfort instead sees "an African substratum of Egyptian culture...the stratum we are looking for is to be found, in fact, in modern Africa underneath later deposits" (451-452). His basic premise is that because of a common origin the people of ancient Egypt and those of other parts of Africa, "extending up to Somaliland" (452), have similar cultural conventions. Comparing the cultures of ancient Egypt, of the Puntites, and of the Masai, he notes the following similarities:

> a particular mode of circumcision...(452)

> a particular method of time reckoning... (452)

> the head dress of the Kings from the fourth dynasty, the *nemes*, head-cloth made to fit a coiffure like that of the Masai warrior... (452)

> "the Puntites had distinctive rigid appendages at the edge of their coiffures... they wore their hair, therefore, as the modern warriors do...." (447-448)

> The archaic garment worn by the king at the Sed festival, and used in the first Dynasty, tallies in length, shape, and far as the pictures allows one to judge, material, with the leather cloaks worn by Masai elders...." (452)

Diffusionist Theory

Seligman, Thomas, Jeffreys and others were advocates of the diffusionist theory, which imputes "influences" from "higher centers of cultures" on lower levels of cultures (Renfrew & Bahn 1991, 408). Today archaeologists generally do not use this explanation for resemblances of cultures. The present-day view is reflected by Renfrew & Bahn (1991), who state that "Today, it is felt that this explanation has sometimes been overplayed and nearly always oversimplified. For although contact between areas, not least through trade, can be of great significance for the developments in each area, the effects of this contact have to be considered in detail: explanation simply in terms of diffusion is not enough" (409).

Jeffreys (1948), who wrote extensively on commonalities of African cultures and Kemet, addresses critics of diffusion. He notes that Western scholarship does not dispute the diffusion of Babylonian culture to the United States. He relates a passage from a textbook concerning:

> the division of the circle into three hundred and sixty degrees, of the day into twenty-four (originally twelve) hours, of the hour into sixty minutes, of the foot into twelve inches, and the pound—as it survives in our Troy weight—into twelve ounces...The Babylonian degrees, minutes, and seconds became an integral part of the ancient astronomy, were taken up by the Greeks, incorporated by them in their development of the system of astronomy known as Ptolemaic, and thus became a part of Roman, Arab, and mediaeval European science. (45)

As Jeffreys comments, "no one boggles about this diffusion of an aspect of Babylonian culture. The point to note is that when things are measured, not counted, a duodecimal notation is used" (45). Another point to note is that the value of Roman, Arab, and European science is not considered diminished because they have borrowed from Babylonian culture.

The point of presenting the information contained in the above articles is not to argue for the value of diffusion theory. The diffusion theory is grounded in a linear Eurocentric paradigm that classifies and places more to be superior. Historian C.T. Keto asserts the importance of the Nile Valley to Africa:

> Drawing from pre-dynastic and dynastic ideas of African religion, government, medicine, architecture and agriculture, later developments and social accomplishments among people of African descent are analyzed in an interconnected temporal context rather than on the basis of extreme diffusionist model. I firmly believe that an Africa-centered perspective on history cannot be sustained as a systematic field of study without its connection to the ancient African cultures of the Nile Valley. (1992, 38)

The holistic approach that our analysis undertakes negates the practice of dividing Africa. Such division clouds a profound understanding of African culture and warps history. Keto states that "The sectionalist focus on sub-Saharan or tropical Africa ignores the cultural interactions in Africa before the desiccation of the Sahel (Sahara) in historical time and the advent of Islam in the seventh century of the Current Era" (38). I postulate that the information concerning cultural similarities found first in the Nile Valley and later in other African cultures reflects different expressions of cultural practices that were developed during historical contacts that African people experienced before the desiccation of the Sahel, and afterwards through trade.

The Sahara was once a fertile area inhabited by African people who have since dispersed. We know that traces of the paleolithic have been found in all of the periods of African prehistory (Diop 1989, 58). Historian Basil Davidson paints a picture of a much different Sahara from the one to which we are now accustomed:

> [T]here should be noted an important natural difference between the Africa of New Stone

> Age times and the Africa of today. West Africa today is divided from North Africa and the Nile by the Sahara Desert. But this was not always the case; in New Stone Age times, this vast and often terrible desert was a rich and fertile land. The Sahara then was clothed with tall trees and green pastures. Broad rivers flowed through it. Game and cattle were plentiful there. Fish abounded.... (1966, 11)

This verdurous Sahara was also teeming with African *people*.

> From one end of the Sahara to the other, from Mauritania in the west to Egypt in the east, scientists have found stone tools and bone harpoons and fishing hooks, as well as pictures and drawings on rock of animals and men and gods. All these were made and left behind by many settlements and groups of vanished people. *The Old Sahara may indeed be reasonably seen as a cradle of early African civilization. Far from being a natural barrier between the peoples of West and North Africa, the Old Sahara joined these peoples together. All could share in the same ideas and discoveries* [emphasis added]. (11)

The evidence also points to the fact that these Africans travelled throughout the Sahara area, particularly the Sahel. Two trails have been found. Davidson reports that "One of these trails passed through Mauritania in the Western Sahara, while the other went though the central Sahara between the middle section of the Niger river and modern Tunisia. *We can be sure that new ideas and discoveries were taken back and forth by these old travellers*" [emphasis added] (12).

The use of data gathered by advocates of diffusion should not be taken as acceptance of their Eurocentric orientations. The present writer uses that data because we can no longer study many of the cultural practices used by African people before colonialism. These practices can be used to demonstrate cultural similarities among African people. Asante, in defining Africology, stresses the importance of the framework of the inquiry. He states that "The scholar who generates research questions based on the centrality of Africa is engaged in a very different research inquiry than the one who imposes Western criteria on the phenomena" (1990, 14). The task of Afrocentric scholarship on Africa is to release knowledge concerning Africa from the bulwark of Eurocentrism. This necessitates recentering information on Africa.

The influx of Islam and Christianity has resulted in the destruction of much of African culture that would be valuable in the analysis of cultural commonalities. For example, in an article in 1916 in *The Journal of Egyptian Archaeology* concerning "Some Remarks On An Emblem Upon The Head Of An Ancient Egyptian Birth-Goddess," Aylward M. Blackman finds it remarkable that in:

> ...part of the famous series depicting the conception and birth of queen Hatshepsut, a goddess who kneels behind the recently delivered mother and extends towards her in either hand the symbol of life...wears on her head an object...which is remarkably like the reliquary...that contains the umbilical cord-stump of the king of Uganda. The fact that an object, identical in shape with the decorated cord-stump of a Baganda king, should appear on the head of an Egyptian goddess closely associated with birth, may be something more than a coincidence." (201-202)

Blackman's article contains an illustration of the goddess depicted in queen Hatshepsut's series as well as photographs of a decorated umbilical cord-stump from the Bagandas of Uganda. However, he notes that another scholar, Roscoe, had a problem in obtaining Ugandan specimens because the "old men have buried many of these sacred relics, to prevent their falling into the possession of Europeans, and to protect them from destruction at the hands of the rising generation, which for the most part, has embraced Christianity or Islam" (201). The destruction of African culture due to assaults by Europeans and Europeanized Africans makes the rewriting of African history a challenging task indeed. Thus, it is necessary to recenter information about cultural practices no longer available through direct observation.

Were one to look at Africa with eyes as wide open as those that look at European culture, then one would expect trade and intercommunications to occur among cultures. When people communicate with each other, practices *will* be borrowed, and adapted to the benefit of the borrower's culture. Moreover, many African ethnic groups consistently speak of a common origin. Diop explains:

> No matter where we collect legends on the genesis of a Black People, those who still remember their origins say they came from the east...Dogon and Yoruba legends report that they came from the east, while those of the Fang...indicate the northeast. For people living south of the Nile, traditions suggest that they came from the north; this is true of the Batutsi of Rwanda-Urundi. When the first sailors to reach the South African disembarked at the Cape several centuries ago, the Zulu, after a north-south migration, had not yet reached the tip of the Cape.

This hypothesis squares with the fact that the tradition of Blacks in the Nile Valley mention only a local origin. Throughout Antiquity, Nubians and Ethiopians never claimed any other, unless it were one farther south....(179)

Thus the legends of many African people point to an eastern origin around the "Great Water" which we can assume is the Nile River. An epistemology centered in African culture informs us that legends are a valid way of knowing. As Asante has said of the issue of epistemology, "In Africalogy, language, myth, ancestral memory, dance-music-art, and science provide the sources of knowledge, the canons of proof and the structures of truth" (1990, 10). The purpose of the placement of Kemet as the classical culture of Africa is to center African history. Without a classical culture, "the history of Black Africa will remain suspended in air and cannot be written correctly" (Diop [1955] 1974, xiv). The identification of Kemet as Africa's classical culture also assists us in understanding the deep structure of other African cultures. It provides a fulcrum for the placement of African cultures. It provides cultural continuity. It does not devalue other African cultures, any more than acknowledging that Europe borrowed a measurement system from the Babylonians devalues European culture. Europe remains the supreme culture, in the minds of Europeans, even though its classical culture, Greece, has many similarities with Africa (James 1954; Bernal 1987; Asante 1990). Yet Afrocentric scholars are criticized when they seek to place African cultures on a par with other cultures. Egyptologists are reluctant to release their hegemonic grip on all matters and materials pertaining to ancient Egypt. Their methods have changed to meet new challenges. No longer can Egyptologists convene and repeat the same old dogma without challenge from Afrocentric scholars. Thus, they have made their attempts to retain supremacy more sophisticated.

We will examine some of the cultural practices that Diop suggested reflect cultural commonalities among all Africans. The first practice that we will examine in detail is the concept of divine kingship.

NOTES

1. This would have been an absurd concept to the Kemites. The people of Greece, Crete, and Syria were always portrayed as foreigners. However, the people of Punt were referred to as their ancestors. Not only were the people of Kush *not* foreigners but they *were* rulers of the 25th dynasty, one of the most cherished in Kemetic history.

2. The throwing stick is very significant to understanding Kemetic cosmogony. "The Throwing Sticks seem to have been personified into an actual deity, for there was a god called "Repeller of Evil."...The Pyramid Texts (#1150) actually use the throwing stick in spelling the word..."hail." Hail is a missile from the sky, and at times a dangerous one...included in the divine armory. Hence, like the others, the Throwing Stick is a suitable simile for the "weapon" of the sky-god (Wainwright 1932:162).

CHAPTER FIVE

DIVINE KINGSHIP

Diop proposes that "[t]he concept of kingship is one of the most impressive indications of the similarity in thinking between Egypt and the rest of Black Africa" (138). In this chapter, we will survey the concept of divine kingship and the manner in which it functions in African cultures. The Kushite culture will then be studied through the concept of divine kingship.

Nubian Origins of Divine Kingship

Of the many scholars who have written about African parallels to divine kingship, one of its strongest proponents was Henri Frankfort. Frankfort directed the Oriental Institute of Chicago's excavation in Iraq from 1929 to 1937, from which he gathered new information on the early history of Babylonia (from 4000 to 2000 B.C.E.). In 1932, he was appointed Research Professor at the University of Chicago. In 1949, he was appointed Director of the Warburg Institute and Professor of the History of Pre-classical Antiquity in the University of London (1956:iv). Frankfort speculated that

> Obviously, kingship was not created in a void, and the unification of the country can be viewed as a short process extending over a few generations. Scorpion is a known conqueror. *There must have been prehistoric chieftains of the type of the Africa rainmaker-king."* [emphasis added] (1948, 18)

The material evidence to support his supposition was not found until 1962 and then only as a consequence of the University of Chicago's Oriental Institute's Nubian Expedition.

In 1962 an expedition team, directed by Keith Seele of the Oriental Institute of Chicago, set out to salvage ancient remains threatened to be damaged by the rising of the Aswan Dam (Williams 1980, 14). Before the results could be published, Seele died. The publication of the results were taken over by archeologist Bruce Williams, who had received his Ph.D. in Near Eastern Archeology from the University of Chicago. Williams, who had believed in a north-south origin of divine kingship, revised his views because of the evidence the team found. "A newly discovered ancient kingdom," he observed, "is always a matter of intense interest, but when it precedes the earliest known monarchy, the unification of Egypt in the fourth millennium B.C., then *history itself is reborn"* [emphasis added] (1980, 12). The team found evidence from the Predynastic period, all previous evidence of which was fragmentary and speculative.

Evidence of the origins of kingship in the Nile Valley was found in Qustal in Lower Nubia. The remains of the people who provided this evidence were part of the so-called A-group, the group already identified by Reisner as being culturally similar to the ancient Kemites, but regarded as lacking in the ability to form their own culture (Reisner 1923, vol.5, 8). This accepted but limited view of these ancient African people was challenged by Williams' interpretation of the new evidence unearthed by the expedition.

The Qustal collection produced "more than 1,000 complete and fragmentary painted pots, and over 100 stone vessels. The range of these and other fragments from the plundered cemetery began to indicate a wealth and complexity that could only be called royal" (Williams 1980, 14). This accumulation of wealth, had it been found in Europe or the Mediterranean, would have been a clear indication of kingship; but because it was found in Nubia, it was contested (16). In fact, archeologist Michael Hoffman does not even mention this important find in his *Egypt Before the Pharaohs* (1979); even though he devoted four chapters to exploring the origins of divine kingship. One of the methods Eurocentric scholars use to "abuse positions of power on questions of knowledge" (Asante 1990, 4) is by deliberate banishment of those viewpoints which differ from the ruling ideology. In the following passage, Williams addresses this problem:

> Tombs of this size, wealth and date in Egypt would have been immediately recognized as royal. Their varied contents would have been taken as evidence of a complex culture exposed to wide outside connections. But because the discovery was made in Nubia at a time and place when kingship was thought impossible, further proof of royalty is a necessity. (16)

Divine kingship and the origins of Kemet are inextricably intertwined. The placement of the monarchy in Nubia *before* it appears in Kemet could also place the *origins* of the people of ancient Egypt in the south. This could lead to the conclusion that the Kemites were Black or at least had origins in common with Black people. Williams' hypothesis had to be confronted and contested by the Egyptological establishment, thus bearing out Cheikh Anta Diop's earlier ([1967] 1974) observation that "The birth of Egyptology was...marked by the need to destroy the memory of a Negro Egypt at any cost and in all minds. Henceforth, the common denominator of all theses of the Egyptologists, their close relationship and profound affinity, can be characterized as a desperate attempt to refute that opinion. Almost all Egyptologists stress its falsity as a matter of course" (45). Williams, who was aware that he was challenging orthodox knowledge, needed more material evidence than the size and content of the tombs to support his theory. He found it in the form of incense burners.

> ...[C]rucial supporting evidence was on hand in the form of the incense burners incised with serekhs, the representations of paneled palace facades. Definitive symbols of Egyptian royalty, serekhs appear in the late Predynastic times often surmounted by the falcon-Horus symbol of the Pharaoh; later they are used to enclose Horus names of Egyptian pharaohs, the major royal name used during the first and second Dynasties. (16)

This incense burner was found in a very rich tomb in cemetery L, which dated back "*six or seven generations before the start of the First Dynasty.*"(16) It is significant to the holistic understanding of African culture that the evidence found in Nubia was in the form of incense burners. Incense has been used extensively in the context of African spirituality. It was considered essential in communications with the gods. One can only recall how much it pleased Maát-Ka-Re Hatshepsut to sponsor the expedition that first brought back the prized myrrh trees from Punt. She had them planted at her temple dedicated to Amon-Re, named Zeser Zeserou. The Qustal collection contained one particular incense burner which Williams described as "the largest, finest and most elaborately decorated of all the A-Group incense burners."(16)

This incense burner was found in its proper context. Williams (1987) specifies that "all of the objects from cemetery L can be assigned to its few tombs and loci." (22) More importantly, there were many symbols of royalty on what Williams has termed "The Horus Incense Burner":

> In the first ship...*the white crown of Upper Egypt* clearly stands out above the ship. In front of it is *the tail of a falcon*—another sign of kingship....In front of the falcon is a *rosette*, a symbol of royalty before the First Dynasty....Its date provided by context, style and composition, the Qustul burner furnishes the earliest definite representation of a king in the Nile Valley or anywhere. [emphasis added] (18)

The early date was also determined by the presence of the following figures: a feline deity; a man saluting in a pose similar to paintings on vases from the Naqada II period; and an antelope and a carnivore frolicking beside a royal ship (18). There were other items unearthed which provided even more evidence "that began to indicate a sequence that led generation from generation from cemetery L to the time of the last pre-First Dynasty tombs at Abydos" (18). This provides very weighty evidence for the placement of the concept of divine kingship in Nubia. The concept of divine kingship is found throughout Africa (Diop [1955] 1974; Seligman 1938; Frankfort 1948) and now it can be shown that the concept began in Nubia, and only subsequently appeared in Kemet.

There was evidence of kingdoms in Nubia before this expedition. One example, cited by Bruce Williams, is a large Sheikh Suleigman monument located south of Qustul. It has been attributed to the first dynasty Kemetic pharaoh Djer, based on his Horus name in a serekh. However, what has been ignored or misinterpreted is the Horus name itself. It is "actually part of an animal common in rock graffiti in Nubia. In fact there is no room for a name on this serekh, and it must be dated with the other unlabeled ones to the Predynastic period....[One enemy] is being physically bound...by a bow, which is significant because the "Land of the Bow" is the earliest hieroglyphic name for Nubia...the bow marks this [as] an A-Group rather than an Egyptian monument."(19)

Ta-Seti, which means "The Land of the Bow" in ancient Egyptian hieroglyphics, was a state with a monarchy. The symbol of the bow appears on monuments, seals, and objects throughout Nubia. One seal described by Williams contains a delineation of a king, known by the palace *serekh*. The *serekh* was previously misinterpreted as a plant because of a crack and an Eurocentric paradigm that was unwilling to acknowledge kingship in Nubia. Williams describes this seal:

> Although a number of aspects of this seal are still difficult to verify, certain features of the iconography are fairly certain, including representations of incense burners in use; D-shaped altars or pylons associated with the Heb-Sed festival, the jubilee celebrated by a pharaoh...and a man seated in a chair saluting the bow symbol...the bow hovers over a shortened rectangle which is saluting the name for Nubia-Ta-Seti, or "Land of the Bow"—as a kingship and territorial state. Obviously, Nubia was a sophisticated political order of an actual and not embryonic rule. (19)

This information confirmed views long held by Black scholars (DuBois 1916; Jackson 1970; Diop 1955). Ivan Van Sertima, editor of the *Journal of African Civilization*, published Williams' article in *Egypt Revisited* (1989). This article and the one published in the *New York Times* ("Nubian Monarchy Called Oldest," 1 March 1979) informed many who do not read the journal *Archeology*. The attention Williams received from Afrocentric scholars and his unorthodox premise also alerted those who sought to maintain the *status quo* in Egyptology. The most prominent attack on Bruce Williams' hypothesis was by William Y. Adams, considered to be the foremost expert on Nubia. Adams wrote an article in *The Journal of Near Eastern Studies* (1985) entitled "Doubts About The 'Lost

Pharaohs.'" Adams (1985) begins by discussing the attention that Williams received:

> Bruce Williams has issued a provocative challenge. He proposes nothing less than a Nubian origin for the immemorial pharaonic monarchy of Egypt....Not surprisingly, it has been welcomed by African nationalists of the Anta Diop [sic] school and has received a wide, if uncritical popular acceptance. (185)

It appears that Adams is somewhat disconcerted by the notice and high regard that Williams is receiving for his theory. Adams argues that:

> ...the Qustal censer proves only that a pharaonic monarchy was in existence somewhere in the Nile Valley at the time of its manufacture. It does not prove, that the monarchy was situated in Nubia rather than in Egypt, or that it predated the earliest rulers of whom we otherwise have evidence. (187)

Adams questions the validity of the evidence. At a conference at the University of Pennsylvania called "Egypt's Rival in Africa" in 1993 (which this researcher attended) the consensus among the presenting scholars (who included Adams) was that the incense burner was a gift or trade item from the Egyptians to the Nubians.

Adams' critique against Williams was written with the virulence usually reserved for Afrocentric scholars. Adams claims that:

> Many of the objections that I have stated here are not original with me. They have previously been voiced by B. Bothmer in *Meroitica*, by A. Spalinger in a letter to the editor of *Archeology*, and by B. G. Trigger,

T. Save-Soderbergh, D. O'Connor, and several other colleagues in private communications....(192)

Adams agrees with the aforementioned Egyptologists not because they share the same discipline, but because they share the same Eurocentric world-view. They all separate Egypt from the rest of Africa, believe that the Egyptians are not Black, and work to conserve the supremacy of Europe. Adams ends this article by claiming his dedication to science, the demi-god of Eurocentricity:

> *My fundamental commitment, however, is to science*...the American Anthropological Association adopted a statement of policy ...that significant theoretical conclusions should not be published apart from, and in advance of, the evidence from which they were derived. I think that the wisdom of that policy is well demonstrated by the A-Group monarchy controversy. (192)

The clear implication is that Adams is disputing Williams' reputation as a credible scientist. For Eurocentric scholars this is the ultimate challenge.

Bruce Williams responds to Adams' challenge in the same journal in an article entitled "Forebears of Menes in Nubia: Myth or Reality?" (*Journal of Near Eastern Studies*, vol. 46, no. 1, 15-26). This title would seem to be a purposeful appropriation of Diop's *The African Origin of Civilization: Myth or Reality* ([1955] 1974), designed to tweak the Eurocentric scholastic community. Williams, in the process of solidly defending his position, provides more evidence concerning the origins of kingship in the Nile Valley.

Williams contends that he did not claim a Nubian origin for ancient Egyptian pharaonic monarchy. His words were more precise than that untenable statement. He selected words such as "participation" and "helped fashion pharaonic civilization" (15). Williams asserts that "*the unification of Nubia preceded that of Upper Egypt*, for cemetery L can be shown to precede the known monuments of the Thinite period at Abydos and the Siali seal names its territory, at least in part" [emphasis added] (16). This is his main claim. The inhabitants of the early Nubia, the so-called A group, were considered to be incapable of monarchy. This hypothesis began with Reisner (1910) and continued into modern times.

Williams proposes that there are cultural links in the iconography which he refers to as "a series of reciprocal interconnections" (17). But African historiography, founded as it is on Hegelian principles regarding Africa, does not seek links in African culture. Hence, those who are ready to disagree with his claims are legion. Williams however, knowing the foundation of the opposition, declares that scholars have been using the so-called A-Group to distort history:

> All of the links to early Egypt are to be abandoned or to be attributed to the export of goods long obsolete in Egypt so that [the] A-Group can be used to plug the gap. *Chronological methods of this sort, that arbitrarily dismiss important bodies of evidence, belong to an age when broad assumptions of "cultural retardation" went unchallenged....*[emphasis added]. (17)

Williams even acknowledges that he began his research "with the same assumptions held by many others in the field at the time." Those assumptions, however, were destroyed, one by one, as the special significance of almost every aspect of the cemetery L overwhelmed them, and they were replaced by the views in 'The Lost Pharaohs of Nubia.' I still advocate those views—if anything, more strongly" (26).

Arguments Against Nubian Origins Of Divine Kingship

The scholastic discourse concerning divine kingship involves the issue of the origins of the Kemetic people. Unquestionably, the dynastic system had very ancient origins. Appropriately, theories concerning those origins have been rife since the beginning of the discipline of Egyptology. Archeologist George Reisner's speculation that "much of Nubia's later prehistory [the Predynastic and so-called A-group phase] was a pale reflection of *developments to the north*, bears on a broader ethnological argument about *the possible African origins of Egyptian kingship*" [emphasis added] (Hoffman 1979, 253). George Reisner is considered the archeologist who laid the foundation for the interpretation of Nubian culture. In fact, anthropologist Michael Hoffman in *Egypt Before The Pharaohs* (1979) refers to Reisner as "the most successful and skilled archeologist of his day" (249). There is no book written about Nubia—as far as our research could determine—that does not refer to Reisner's work. Although the quality of his excavations cannot be denied, all material remains must be interpreted, and Reisner's interpretations were far from objective and ultimately asserted the superiority of an Eurocentric world-view. Not surprisingly, his outcomes do not support an Afrocentric perspective and, certainly, to serve this perspective was not his intention.

Reisner's influence is so enduring because he laid the foundation for archeological excavation as it is practiced today. An examination of the principles he developed will help explain the extent of his power. Those principles were: the necessity of having an organized staff of Europeans, who oversee indigenous workmen; excavation of whole sites and cemeteries, which are taken off layer by layer in inverse order; the maintenance of precise records and photographs which must be published (252). The above procedures are now considered to be standard operations for archeological excavations, and it was Reisner who set these standards. Reisner was named the director of the first large-scale salvage campaign, the erection of the Aswan Dam in 1907. Reisner's conclusions were based on the analysis of fifty-eight cemeteries.

About the earliest inhabitants of Kemet Reisner postulated that "The Badarian epoch as yet unrecognized in Upper Egypt, was apparently absent from Lower Nubia, suggesting that this early farming culture *must have originated north of Aswan* and that the center of earliest Predynastic development was in Egypt proper" (Hoffman 1979, 255). Reisner thus set the stage for disconnecting Kemet from the rest of Africa:

> The earliest population were shown by their skeletons to be of the same proto-Egyptian race as the predynastic Egyptians: their pottery, their flint and stone implements, their store of ores and metal objects, their stone vessels, their tanned skins, their cloth and matting, their ornaments and amulets of stone, ivory, and faience, were identical in material, form, and technique with the same objects of the same period found in Egypt ....(Reisner 1923 [a] V:5)

Similarities in bone structure, tools, ornaments, clothing would rather seem, to this writer, to constitute evidence of cultural similarities between the people of Egypt and those of Nubia. Reisner was not seeking relationships; instead, confronted with evidence of cultural commonalities, he began the process of separating them. Placing a lower value on Nubia, he concludes that "the lagging behind of the Nubian communities and the independent development of their one prominent local industry, pottery, was accompanied by an increasing change in the racial character of the people. *The negroid element became more marked*" [emphasis added] (ibid, 6). Reisner separates Kemet and Nubia into superior and inferior cultures based solely on the criterion of race (as he defines it). He asserts that "The people in these poor Nubian graves of the Old Kingdom show considerable anatomical differences from those of the preceding period; but *they are not negroes as we use the term to-day. They are, however, negroid and not Egyptian* [emphasis added]" (ibid.). In this, Reisner is deferring to G. Elliot Smith as *the* authority on the race of the Nubians, for it was Smith who had designated this race as "Old Nubian...*it is quite clear that they are not negroes*" [emphasis added] (Reisner 1923, 6). (The characteristics of these skeletons which make them "definitely not negro," however, is never specified. His judgement in this matter is simply not questioned, even today.) Accordingly, Reisner (1923) insisted that civilization in the Nile Valley should be understood in terms of a north-to-south migration:

> ...[A] race was revealed which...was racially and culturally descended from the people living in the same place in the Old Kingdom. This Nubian race was negroid, but not negro; it was perhaps a mixture of the proto-Egyptian and a negro or negroid race, possibly related to the Libyan race. It lay outside the cultural influence of Egypt and, seeming to lack power or the opportunity of self-culture....(8)

Building on Reisner's assessment that the Nubians had no cultural correlations with Kemet, Hoffman denies that divine kingship had African origins. In the process, he cites numerous experts on the subject in order to substantiate his position:

> Perhaps the single most distinctive trait of ancient Egyptian civilization was the concept of divine kingship. It was the ideological glue that held the early state together and... there is considerable evidence that it developed out of a pre-historic antecedent ....(257)

Continuing his argument, Hoffman cites Bruce Trigger, a highly respected archeologist, who "summed up the limited horizons of chieftainship in Lower Nubia in Protodynastic times" (260). Trigger, like Hoffman, uses the power of definition to build his argument. Trigger does not identify the Nubians as kings, instead calling them chiefs. He states that "The Nubian chiefs probably controlled much of the trade with Egypt...and hence stood at the apex of small redistributive systems in their own country....Some of these men may have been skillful politicians who were able to collect tribute or taxes....In any case the power which any of these chiefs had must have been severely limited both in terms of area and authority" (260). Trigger is unable to envision a concept of kingship in ancient Nubia. Prior to the unification of Kemet by Menes, the rulers of Kemet apparently ruled over limited areas, yet they are referred to as kings. The powers to control trade, collect taxes, and control redistribution systems are indicative of early state societies (*Archeology* 1991, 155). These early rulers of Nubia were definitely controlling trade and seemed to control redistribution. Whether the rulers of these early state societies are 'chiefs' or 'kings' is purely a matter of definition.

William Adams is similarly reluctant to define these early Nubian rulers as kings. He refers to "rulers of Yam." The exact location of Yam is unclear, although it is definitely in Nubia. Adams writes:

> *Nowhere in the archeological record of Lower Nubia are we confronted with the recognizable trappings of monarchy: neither palaces nor royal tombs nor conventional royal insignia. Yet Egyptian texts from the VI Dynasty onward are full of references to Nubian rulers....Nearly a dozen localities are mentioned in connection with 'chiefs' in one context or another.* (1977, 158)

The above quote gives us an indication of the reason why divine kingship in Nubia had been unrecognized before the

Chicago Oriental Institute's Nubian expedition. It was not because there was no evidence before, but because the scholars who were interpreting the evidence had a limited vision. A lack of archeological evidence has never meant that something did not exist. It does mean that the seekers of evidence may not have been looking in the right places; or it may mean that when they found the evidence they misinterpreted it. The ancient texts are clear. There were powerful rulers in this area.

Hoffman builds on his argument against a southern foundation of divine kingship when he states that "if the institution of divine kingship had evolved from a more general African context, then we should be able to trace its more or less parallel emergence among many fourth millennium B.C. farming and herding societies along the Nile" (261). The present writer contends that those with this world-view cannot see kingship in Nubia because they are unwilling to conceptualize cultural commonalities in Africa.

Constituents of Divine Kingship

Diop cites two characteristics of kingship that are particular to African cultures: (1) the sacrosanct nature of kingship and (2) the ritual killing of the king. On the sacrosanct nature of kingship Diop writes:

> The king is the demiurge Ra, on Earth, who mirrors and perpetuates creation; he is the intermediary between God (his father) and humanity, and as such, *he guarantees cosmic order* [emphasis added]. ([1981] 1991, 334)

The principal role of the king was to maintain cosmic order, called *Maát*. Molefi Asante (1990) is in agreement with Diop when he writes that "the kings of Egypt were not merely kings, they were the embodiment of the concept of Maát, and the goddess Maát stood with them so long as they stood with Maát" (90). Maát is the oldest known ethical and spiritual system in the world. The political aspect of kingship was of very little significance to the concept of kingship. Anthropologist Henri Frankfort in his book *Kingship and the Gods* (1948) describes how the people of Kemet perceived the role of the king:

> ...[I]f we refer to kingship as a political institution, we assume a point of view which would have been incomprehensible to the ancients....*The ancients, however, experienced human life as part of a widely spreading network of connections which reached beyond the local and the national communities into the hidden depths of nature and the powers that rule nature....*Whatever was significant was imbedded in the life of the cosmos, and it was precisely the king's function to maintain the harmony of that integration. [emphasis added] (3)

Pharaoh had power over the seen and the unseen. He was indispensable to the divine order of the universe. This extended into his death and explains the significance of the pyramids. Those who participated in the building of the pyramids contributed to divine order. They gained reciprocal benefits that empowered them.

Frankfort declares that "Pharaoh was not a mortal but a god. This was the fundamental concept of Egyptian kingship, that Pharaoh was of divine essence, a god incarnate: and this view can be traced back as far as texts and symbols take us" (5). The symbols on the Horus Incense Burner demonstrate that the king was regarded as divine. Pharaoh did not *become* a god, Pharaoh simply *was* a god. Frankfort (1948) is very explicit when he states that "His divinity was not proclaimed at a certain moment, in a manner comparable to the *consecratio* of the dead emperor by the Roman senate. *His coronation was not an apotheosis but an epiphany*" [emphasis added] (5). This is very distinctly African, different not only from the aforementioned Romans, but also from the Mesopotamians, with whom the ancient Egyptians are often compared. Frankfort argues that:

> ...[T]here is a complete contrast between Egypt and Mesopotamia. The earliest Mesopotamia term for king...Sumerian *lugal* means "great man." The Mesopotamian king was, like Pharaoh, charged with maintaining harmonious relations between human society and the supernatural powers; yet he was emphatically not one of these but a member of the community. In Egypt, on the other hand, one of the gods had descended among men. (6)

The currency of belief in ancient Egypt can be verified in many ways, one of which is the matrilineal system. Pharaohs traced lineage through the mother only, possibly because the father of the king was assumed to be a deity. One of the most vivid depictions can be found on the walls of Hatshepsut's mortuary temple, Zeser Zeserou, in which one can see her mother queen Ahmose having sexual intercourse with Amon-Re, which resulted in the birth of Hatshepsut. Another indication is the method in which the Kemites depicted Pharaoh. He is always depicted as a towering figure who single-handedly conquers enemies, as on the famous Narmer palette. This palette, like all African art, can be understood on various levels. Frankfort declares that "The enemies...represent an element of chaos.... Victory is not merely assertion of power; it is the reduction of chaos to order." (9)

The Kemites did not expect Pharaoh to abuse power even though it was assumed that he had unlimited power. The reason was Maát. This is key to the understanding of the deep structure of divine kingship. Maát permeated various levels of the society.

From very ancient times the Maáti were two goddesses, Auset and Nabhet, who represented the ideas of "straightness, integrity, righteousness, what is right, the truth and so forth, the word Maát originally meant measuring stick" (Budge 1904, xx). This concept of Maát is "of very great antiquity in Egypt: indeed it is so old that it is useless to try to ascertain the date of the period when it first grew up" (115). Maát was associated with eternal life. If Pharaoh wanted eternal life he had to rule in accordance with the principles of Maát. The deceased, after having recited prayers and adorations to Re, the omnipotent deity, and to his son, Osar, next came into the Hall of Maáti in order that he/she may be "separated from every sin which he has done, and may behold the faces of the gods" (*The Book of the Dead*, Chap. 125).

The original Hall of Maáti contained forty-two deities who judged the deceased. The deceased would enumerate the offenses he/she had not committed, commonly known as the Negative Confessions, in front of each of the deities. The deceased then concluded by making a Declaration of Innocence: "I am pure, I am pure; I am pure; I am pure." The heart of the deceased was then weighed on a scale against a feather, which was the symbol of Maát. Maát was a way of life.

> In the...Hall of Maáti, is set a balance wherein the heart of the deceased is to be weighed. The beam is suspended by a ring upon a projection from the standard of the balance made in the form of a feather which is the symbol of Maát, or what is right and true. The tongue of the balance is fixed to the beam, and when this is exactly level, the tongue is as straight as the standard (Budge 1904, 135-136).

The weighing of the heart was a process in which one's positive deeds were weighed against one's negative deeds. One's positive deeds must balance the feather of Maát. The ancient Egyptians recognized that life is always a struggle between good and evil. Therefore:

> ...It must be distinctly understood that...all that was asked or required of the deceased

was that his heart should balance exactly the symbol of the law. (Budge 1904, 135-136)

The role of the ruler was to balance the activities of the state so that Maát would be achieved. This was a process not an outcome. It became an ethical system which guided the activities of the king. It was not expected that the ruler would never make a mistake, but that order would be achieved through the balance of things toward the good.

The Ritual Killing of the King

The ritual killing of the king is related to the respect for life that is inherent in Africans. Diop provides insight into this custom:

> The monarch...was also supposed to be the man with the greatest life force or energy. When the level of his life force fell below a certain minimum, it could only be a risk to his people if he continued to rule. This vitalistic conception is the foundation of all traditional African kingdoms....(138)

The ritual killing of the king has been examined extensively by Scottish anthropologist James George Frazer, author of the classic anthropology text, *The Golden Bough* (1921), an extensive survey of the origins of so-called world religions. His work has been assessed negatively by archeologist Michael Hoffman, who professes to represent the consensus of the scientific community. However, Frazer's work is germane to our topic even though it has been viewed negatively by some Eurocentric scholars, as he cites specific cases of regicide in Africa. The information that is contained in his work about African ethnic groups can be recentered and used in an Afrocentric analysis.

Frazer posits that "Man has created gods in his own likeness and being himself mortal he naturally supposed his creatures to be in the same sad predicament" (308). African philosophy places humans at the center of the universe

(Jahn 1961; Mbiti 1969). It is humans who fashion gods after themselves. Kemetic cosmogony demonstrates this point, according to Frazer:

> [The great gods of Egypt] too grew old and died. But when at a later time the discovery of the art of embalming gave a new lease of life to the souls of the dead by preserving their bodies for an indefinite time from corruption, the deities were permitted to share the benefit of an invention which held out to gods as well as to men a reasonable hope of immortality. (308)

Thus, if the gods could die, then the divine human who ruled could only be expected to do the same. The divine ruler represented the life force of the people and nature was dependent of his having a vital life force. He could not be prevented from dying, no matter how much attention and care were given him. This was a very momentous concern. Frazer illuminates this subject:

> There is only one way of averting these dangers. The man-god must be killed as soon as he shows symptoms that his powers are beginning to fail, and his soul must be transferred to a vigorous successor before it has been seriously impaired by the threatened decay. (309-310)

Frazer traces regicide through many cultures, most particularly in Africa, where it occurs with great frequency. In Africa, he cites Meroe, in particular, where it happened in antiquity and has continued in that geographical area through the modern era. He also cites incidences among many African ethnic groups, including the Shilluk in the area of the White Nile; the Dinka of the White Nile area; the Central African kingdom of Bunyoro; the Junkos of the Niger River area; the Hausa kingdoms of Godir, Katsina, and Daura in Northern Nigeria; and the Zulu (310-316).

Frazer includes a direct quotation of someone who lived in the court of Zulu king Chaka Zulu. Chaka became obsessed with obtaining an oil that covered grey hair because it appears it was the custom of the Zulus to put a king to death as soon as his hair turned grey or he wrinkled (316). The killing of the divine king either took place when he showed signs of deteriorating or at the end of a specified term. Frazer declares that "some peoples...appear to have thought it unsafe to wait for even the slightest symptom of decay and have preferred to kill the king while he was still in the full of vigor" (319).

Ethnologist C.G. Seligman (1934) wrestled with the reason why the ritual killing of the king was so significant to African culture. In *Egypt and Negro Africa: A Study in Divine Kingship*, he surmises that:

> ...the complex of beliefs centering round the Divine Kingship must have appealed to some deep-seated need of early West African man...the belief in the connection between fertility and that of the land is very widespread....(18)

Seligman placed his and other researchers' ethnographic information within his concept of the Hamite. He states that in this book he is attempting to "estimate whether the existence of [Divine Kings] is to be regarded as due to *the survival in different parts of Africa of the beliefs of a very old immigrant Caucasian stock, the Hamites, of whom the proto-Egyptians were themselves a branch*, or whether the belief is to be considered as specifically Egyptian in origin and as having spread from Egypt by culture contact" [emphasis added] (3). Unquestionably, he separates the ancient Egyptians from the rest of Africa, referred to as Black Africa. Seligman also does not assume "any early massive contact of the two peoples, though a gradual infiltration of Egyptian ideas into black Africa must have existed from early times, presumably as early as the Pyramid Age" (4). The limited contact to which he does submit is placed within an Eurocentric concept of an assumed superior Caucasian culture, that of ancient Egypt, giving Culture to inferior cultures, the rest of Africa. These concepts need to be reexamined.

However, Seligman's statement concerning the importance of the land—and the connection between the land's fertility and the ruler's role in ensuring it—is valid. For, since the king was responsible for Maát and since the fertility of the land was necessary for balance and order, the decreased vitality of the king would affect the production of the land. This suggests an underlying reason for the ritual killing of the king and the *sed*[1] festival.

The *sed* festival was a momentous time in which Pharaoh revitalized his/her potency (Frankfort 1948, 79). It is important to comprehend the relevance of the *sed* festival in order to grasp the meaning of divine kingship. Seligman maintains that "In the five days of its duration multifarious connections between gods and king, land and king, people and king, were woven into that elaborate fabric which held society as well as the unaccountable forces of nature by strands which passed through the solitary figure on the throne of Horus" (1948, 79). The elaborate ceremony required: that new temples be built, especially for the deity that the king worshipped the most; two buildings, "The Festival Hall," where the Great Throne stood, and the "Palace," in which the king changed costume and insignia; purification rites; the "Lighting of the Flame," (this ritual lasted for five days); barges with deities from all parts of the land; meetings with important officials; "a great procession in which the king, the statues of the gods and priesthood, and the secular participants took part" (80-84). The *sed* dance was a distinctive part of the ceremony. The king dedicated a piece of land to the gods by crossing the length and breadth of it in a series of fast steps (85). The Kemites usually operated on multiple levels. This can be discerned in hieroglyphics and certainly in a ceremony as meaningful as this one. Frankfort suspects, and this researcher agrees, that the land represented the dedication of all of united Kemet to the gods and the declaration of the king's power over the land (86). The festival ends with a tribute to deities associated with Royal Ancestors, thus completing a circle.

The *sed* festival was very ancient. M.A. Murray (1932) described two limestone statuettes found at Hierakonpolis: "the larger of the two...approximates in style to the figure of the Scorpion King, and also to the dancing man of the large mace-head...and is therefore probably of the same period—before Narmer" (70) [see appendix]. Undoubtedly, the roots of the *sed* were predynastic. Murray also states that:

> The two statuettes represent the King and the royal lady (wife or daughter) in the Sed-festival...he conforms to the conventions which were found later. *This shows that the type of representation as well as the actual festival were completely fixed before the historic period* [emphasis added]. (70)

Bruce Williams and Thomas J. Logan of Gibbes Art Museum, Charleston, South Carolina, in their article, "The Metropolitan Museum Knife Handle and Aspects of Pharaonic Imagery Before Narmer" (1987, 245-286), elaborate on a premise postulated by Williams in his "Lost Pharaohs of Nubia" (1987) and recenter some notable pieces of predynastic iconography. They arrived at the conclusion that prior to and continuing into the Dynastic period, there was a "cycle of standard themes" which were indications of the "expected liturgical activities of the ruler" (271). The central event of "the expected duties of leadership" was the *Heb-Sed* (272). The sustained vitality of Pharaoh and the land was of major importance to these ancient Africans. Williams and Logan explain the consistent occurrence of this festival:

> In several representations, the pharaoh is depicted with the bark wearing the Heb-Sed garment. The central tableau in Tomb 100 is the Heb-Sed run or dance, a representation also found in Djoser's substructure....The

Qustal Incense Burner shows where the ceremony took place—at or in a palace-facaded building. (271)

The authors conclude, and this researcher concurs, that "it is now reasonable to ask how much of the art before Narmer is not an abbreviation or extension of the early greater cycle. Is it not possible for Egyptologists to view the concepts of 'prehistoric' and 'pre-Dynastic' as obsolete constructs of late-nineteenth century historiographical predisposition and abandon them now?" (272).

The concept of divine kingship is one of the most pivotal and pronounced cultural commonalities among African people. We will now examine divine kingship in Kush.

Kush and Divine Kingship

The image of the Ethiopian[2] throughout antiquity was one of piousness. In fact, Frank Snowden (1970) informs his readers in *Blacks in Antiquity* that "an image of pious, just Ethiopians became so imbedded in Greco-Roman tradition that echoes are heard throughout classical literature." (144) This image was no doubt caused by the contacts that the Greeks and Romans had with the Ethiopians.

The Greek writer Diodorus Siculus describes the process of the election of kings in Meroe. The text contributes to evidence of the divine nature of kingship in Kush.

> *The priests, for instance, first choose out the noblest men from their own number, and whichever one from this group the god may select*, as he is borne about in a procession in accordance with a certain practice of theirs, him the multitude take for their king: and straightaway *it both worships and honours him like a god, believing that the sovereignty has been entrusted to him by Divine Providence* [emphasis added]. (III, 5)

After being selected, the king then followed in the ways of the ancestors, another cultural practice common throughout Africa. Diodorus states that "And the king who has been thus chosen both follows a regimen which has been fixed in accordance with the laws and performs all his other deeds in accordance with ancestral custom" (III, 5). This practice occurs again in Kushite history when the kings of the 25th dynasty returned to the ways of the ancestors when they attempted to restore Kemet to its former glory.

Strabo, a Greek geographer and historian, concurs that the Ethiopians who lived in Meroe considered the kingship to be divine. Strabo writes that "They regard as god the immortal being, whom they consider the cause of all things, and also the mortal being, who is without name and not to be identified. But in general they regard their benefactors and royal personages as gods: of these the kings are the common saviors and guardians of all, and special individuals as in a special sense gods to those who have received benefactions from them" (XVII, 2, 3).

In Diodorus' writings we also find evidence the Kushites engaged in the cultural practice of the ritual killing of the king. The text of Diodorus reads:

> Of all their customs the most astonishing is that which obtains in connection with the death of their kings. For the priests at Meroe...being the greatest and most powerful order, whenever the idea comes to them, dispatch a messenger to the king, with orders that he die. For the gods...have revealed this to them....Now in former times the kings would obey the priests...but during the reign of the second Ptolemy the king of the Ethiopians, Ergamenes, who had a Greek education and had studied philosophy, was the first to have the courage to disdain the command...he...put the priests to the sword, and after abolishing this custom thereafter ordered affairs after his own will.(III, 6)

Strabo also writes of the same story:

> In Meroe the highest rank in ancient times was held by the priests, who would give orders even to the king, sometimes ordering him....[B]ut later one of the kings did away with this custom, having come with his warriors to the temple, where the gold *noas* stood, and slaughtered all the priests. (XVII, 2, 3)

If these writers are to be believed[3] (and we have evidence that Strabo visited Ethiopia and that Diodorus interviewed Ethiopian ambassadors), then their works can be considered very close to being primary source evidence. The ritual killing of the king was being practiced by these African people.

It is apparent that the culture was not fully understood by these outsiders. Diodorus writes that prior to Ergamenes, the ritual killing of the king was "accepted by the simple mind of a creature shaped by old and ineffaceable customs." The Greek mind separated the material and the spiritual. The spiritual nature of the ritual killing of the king would be incomprehensible to the mind of the ancient Greek. Also, Diodorus believes that this ritual was "senseless orders" and he did not comprehend that the kings in these cases submitted willingly. The king was a god and submitted for the purpose of Maát, or divine order, which had various names throughout Africa. They were held responsible for "right ordering and especially the fertility of the earth and domestic animals" (Seligman 1934, 5). Throughout Africa, kings with such responsibility

> end their lives by being killed or killing themselves with greater or lesser ceremony often at a fixed period (as the oncoming of senescence) or ceremonially expose themselves to the chance of death or else feign to die. *And here it is worth stressing that even under the inhibitory conditions of modern*

> *government the Divine King goes cheerfully to his death* [emphasis added]. (ibid. 6)

We do not know the reason Ergamenes rebelled against the ritual killing by the priests. It may have been his Greek education or perhaps his desire to reduce the power of the priesthood, such as that which may have motivated Akhenaton. For the purposes of this study, these passages provide evidence of divine kingship and the ritual killing of the king. Now we will examine the words of one of the kings of the 25th dynasty for evidence of divine kingship.

Piankhi

Piankhi came to the throne about 741 B.C.E. He has left one of the most thorough, well-known documents from the Nile Valley. In fact Egyptologist and grammarian, Alan H. Gardiner, writes of Piankhi's text that

> For those whose life is devoted to the study of Egyptian texts it is somewhat humiliating to find that some of the most interesting hieroglyphic inscriptions...emanate from the Nubian kings of alien descent who ruled Egypt....(Gardiner 1935, 219)

Gardiner's feeling of humiliation arises solely from the Eurocentric separation of Kush from Kemet. A holistic approach presupposes that the Kushite rulers, who were uniting the Nile Valley, could likewise produce outstanding hieroglyphic documents. Gardiner attributes "the picturesque details and manifestations of personal temperament" (219) to "the foreign blood of an energetic and warlike race" (219). The differences in personalities among kings of England, Rome, Greece, or France—or popes for that matter—are never imputed to differences in race. Yet Gardiner, despite this negative judgment, can still appreciate the magnificence of the text:

> The third Tuthmosis and the second Rameses have afforded us accounts of their exploits far less jejune than those of most of their compatriots. But who among us will prefer their narration to that of the Ethiopian conqueror Piankhi?" (219)

Piankhi begins by informing the reader of his divinity:

> I am king, divine emanation, living image of Atum, who came forth from the womb, adorned as a ruler, of whom those greater than he were afraid: whose father knew, and whose mother recognized that he would rule in the egg, the Good God, beloved of the gods, achieving with his hands, Meriamon-Piankhi. (Breasted 1962, IV, #817, 419)

Piankhi presents a narrative concerning how he came to rule the Nile Valley. Throughout this text he demonstrates his piety and his belief that he was restoring Maát to Kemet.

Piankhi is informed that Tefnakht, a ruler of the Delta city of Sais, "a chief of the west...has seized the whole west from the back-lands to Ithtowe, coming southward with a numerous army, while the Two Lands are united behind him, and the princes and rulers of walled towns are as dogs at his heels. [H]e besieges Heracleopolis, he has completely invested it, not letting the comers—out come out, and not letting the goers-in go in, fighting every day" (#818, 419). Piankhi's response to this information was to laugh with joy. The princes and commanders of the army appealed to him on a daily basis "Wilt thou be silent....While Tefnakhte advances his conquest and finds none to repel his arm" (#819, 420). Another town, Hermopolis, submits to Tefnakhte before Piankhi responds. What Piankhi does next illustrates that he believes that he is in alliance with Amun:

> Then sent His Majesty an army into Egypt charging them very strictly: Attack not the enemy by night...but fight when you can be seen....Fight only when he bids...harness the best steed of thy stable, draw up in line of battle. *For know thou that Amun is the god that hath sent us* [emphasis added]. (Gardiner, 1935; 219)

Piankhi's words advising his army to "attack not the enemy by night" seem like "strange strategical counsel" to Gardiner (220). However, "they bear witness to his high courage and unswerving piety" (220). Indeed, in his instructions to his army, Piankhi expresses his conviction that he is responsible for maintaining Maát:

> When you have reached Thebes...enter into the water, purify yourselves in the river, array yourselves in clean linen (?), rest the bow...*Boast not of being lords of might, for without him no brave hath strength; he maketh strong the weak*, so that many flee before the few, and one man overcometh a thousand. *Besprinkle yourselves with water from his altars. Kiss the earth before his face* [emphasis added]. (220)

The "him" and "he" to which Piankhi refers is Amun. Piankhi is advising his army to maintain spiritual awareness. Success in the battle was not to be attributed to the power of bows, but to the power of the spirit. This was attained by communicating with Amun. As a divine king, Piankhi was fulfilling his charge as a member of the pantheon of the gods. As an upholder of Maát, he was responsible for preserving holistic relationships between the community of humans and the community of the gods.

When the army arrived at the sacred city of Thebes, they "did according to all that his majesty had said," for "who is thy equal therein?" (Breasted 1962, #824-825, 422-423). The divine king had no equal. Unlike Mesopotamia, as Frankfort postulates, where the king was a great man who arose from the people, the divine king was one of the gods who descended to rule the people (1948, 6). Piankhi's men "threw themselves upon their bellies before [him]... saying: It is thy name which endues us with might, and thy counsel is the mooring-post of thy army; thy bread is in our bellies on every march, thy beer quenches our thirst" (Breasted 1962, #824, 422). Bread and beer were symbols for life in the Nile Valley. We meet these symbols again in numerous ritual formulas for offerings that kings give to the gods. Truly, in the eyes of his army, Piankhi had no equal.

Later when Piankhi receives reports that the northern army had been allowed to escape to the Delta, he becomes enraged (ibid., #801, 409). He begins to swear that "as Re loves me! As my father Amon favors me! I will myself go northward..." (#835, 426). However, before Piankhi proceeds to enter the battle himself, he participates in rituals honoring Amon and, no doubt, strengthening his *ka*.

> Now, afterwards when the ceremonies of the New Year are celebrated, I will offer to my father, Amon, at his beautiful feast, when he makes his beautiful appearance of the New Year, *that he may send me forth in peace*, to behold Amon at the beautiful Feast of Opet [emphasis added]. (#836, 426)

Piankhi and his army proceeded to besiege and win Hermopolis from King Namlot. Namlot at first sent messengers with "gold, every splendid costly stone, clothing in a chest, and the diadem which was on his head" to appease Piankhi. This did not achieve the goal. So he "set his wife, the king's wife, and the king's-daughter, Nestent...to plead with the king's-wives, king's-concubines, king's-daughters, and king's-sisters, to throw herself upon her belly in the harem[4] before the king's-wives" (#844, 428). This was a successful tactic. It illustrates the esteemed position of women in Kushite culture. Namlot's use of women to plead his cause suggests that he was aware that Piankhi's wives, daughters, and sisters had his ear and could influence him.

Piankhi then enters Hermopolis. His first act is to make the proper sacrifices to "his father, Thoth, lord of Hermopolis" (#848, 429). This provides balance to military activities, contributes to sacred order, and renders reciprocity to the god that assisted his efforts.

Piankhi visits Namlot's palace where the king presented his women to him. However, Piankhi "turned not his face to them" but "proceeded to the stable of horses" (#849-50, 429). When he observed that the horses were hungry and ill kept, he said:

> I swear, as Re loves me...it is more grievous in my heart that my horses have suffered hunger, than any evil deed that thou hast done....Didst thou not know that the god's shadow is over me? and that my fortune never perishes because of him? Would that another had done it to me!... When I was being fashioned in the womb, and created in the divine egg the seed of the god was in me. By his ka, I do nothing without him; he it is who commands me to do it. (#850, 429-430)

This passage helps us understand why Piankhi places so much value on the horses. Africans impute numerous religious associations to animals. The full significance of horses to the Kushites is not known. It is known that animals symbolize different aspects of the spiritual world (Mbiti [1969] 1990). It is safe to suggest that, based on African culture, horses had more significance than just accoutrements of war. Piankhi, as protector of Maát, was responsible for maintaining the harmony of the material and spiritual order of the universe. Namlot had transgressed upon spiritual order in his treatment of the horses. Piankhi was enraged.

Piankhi remains diligent in his piety. After each conquest, contributions are made to the treasury and granary of Amon. After Memphis was conquered "as (by) a flood of water," he protected the sacred places. The text says that "He...the holy of holies of the gods, offered to the community of gods of Hatkeptah (Memphis), cleansed Memphis with natron and incense, installed the priests in their places" (#865, 435). The text suggests that the re-establishment of Maát was accomplished through the protection of the sacred. Piankhi proceeds to the house of Ptah, where:

> [H]is purification was performed in the Dewat-chamber, and every custom that is practiced upon a king was fulfilled upon him. He entered into the temple, and a great oblation was made for his father, "Ptah-South-of-His-Wall"...consisting of bulls, calves, fowl, and everything good. (#866, 435)

It appears that in each city Piankhi conquered he assumed the primary deity as his divine father. In this manner he established that he had been recognized by the deity as of the divine order. He performed the same ceremony in Khereha in honor of Atum. The ritual that Piankhi performed at the Temple of Re was one of the most critical rituals he could perform. It was a very ancient ceremony. He alone faced Re.

> [H]e entered the temple with great praise... he was purified with incense and libations; garlands for the pyramidion-house were presented to him, and flowers were brought to him. *He ascended the steps to the great window, to behold Re...The king himself stood alone, he broke the bolts, opened the double doors, and beheld his father, Re...* [emphasis added](#871, 436-7)

After liberating Kemet from Tefnakhte and the others, Piankhi returned home. Like other kings in Africa, he was not seen often by the people. The text tells us that:

> "O mighty, mighty Ruler, Piankhi, O mighty Ruler; thou comest, having gained the dominion of the Northland...Happy the heart of the mother who bore thee, and the man who begat thee. Those who are in the valley give to her praise, the cow that hath borne a bull. Thou art unto eternity, thy might endureth, O Ruler, beloved of Thebes." (#883, 443)

Stela of King Taharqa

Taharqa[5], biological son of Piankhi, was born in 708 B.C.E.. He began his reign in 690 B.C.E. at the age of twenty, when he was beckoned by Shabataka (Shebitku) to come to Egypt.

> Now His Majesty had been in Nubia as a goodly youth, a king's brother, pleasant of love, and he came north to Thebes in the company of goodly youths whom His Majesty King Shebitku had sent to fetch from Nubia, in order that he might be there with him, since he loved him more than all his brethren...and his name became Horus Lofty-of-Diadems....Then His Majesty said to his courtiers, "Lo, I desire to rebuild the temple of *my father Amon-Re of Gempaten*" [emphasis added]...(Macadam 1949, 15-16)

It was through this process of selection that Taharqa became king. Taharqa writes of himself as the son of Amon-Re. He perceives himself as having been born divine. His mother, Abar, played an important role during his reign. (Abar's position will be examined in more detail in the chapter on matriarchy.) One of Taharqa's first tasks is to rebuild the temple of his father, Amon-Re. On stela VI of Kawa he declares that "the god was in this place, yet it was not known what the rain had done. But he it was who preserved this temple until it befell that I was crowned King. For he knew that his son, namely I, whom he begat, had made a monument for him" (16). Again in Stela of King Taharqa, Year 10, Taharqa announces that "His Majesty ordered (4) true cedar of Lebanon to be brought southward in order to set up his trees in this temple which His Majesty made for his father Amun....It was he that dug for the cool waters of the altars which satisfy the heart of Amun the Great" (Macadam, 42). In Taharqa, we see an epiphany of the divine order. Like other divine kings, Taharqa portrays himself as the sole slayer of enemies and maintainer of Maát.

> Now His majesty is a master of rejuvenescence, a champion, one uniquely valiant, a strong king without peer, ruling like Atum, the love of him (3) pervading the world like (that of) Re when he shines in the sky, the son of Re...sending for his arrow so that he overcomes the mighty, trampling the hills in pursuit of (5) his foes with fight in his mighty arm, slaying hundreds of thousands ...(IV, 15).

Summary

Through the texts of Greek contemporaries and the king's own stela, this section seeks to contribute to a deeper understanding of divine kingship and how it functioned in Kush. This does not claim to be an exhaustive account. However, through this chapter, one can discern evidence that divine kingship in Kush, Kemet, and other African cultures existed. Divine kingship played a significant role in how Africans perceived the world and their place in it. The 25th Dynasty—the Kushite Rejuvenation Dynasty—was a period when Africans from the south, were acting as self-conscious agents of their own destiny. This was one of the beloved dynasties of Kemetic history. The rulers were divine kings, which is "one of the most impressive indications of the similarity of thinking between Egypt and the rest of black Africa" (Diop [1955] 1974, 139).

NOTES

1. The origins of the name *sed* are uncertain. However, Frankfort (1948) supports one explanation given by Professor Margaret Murray (1904) in *The Osireion at Abydos* (34). She posits that there was a deity named Sed, depicted on the Palermo Stone and in titles of the Old Kingdom. "If Sed were an ancient form of the god Upwaut, his name could appropriately designate a feast of the rebirth of kingship, for Upwaut...was probably a divine form of Pharaoh in his aspect of eldest son and plays a prominent role in the Sed festival." (366) This at least gives us a workable hypothesis.

2. The name Ethiopia was used by classical Greek and Roman writers for the area we refer to as Kush. The boundaries of Ethiopia were inexact, but it was generally agreed to extend from India to West Africa. The word Ethiopia meant "land of people with charred faces" (Vionogradov, *Meroitica*, 1984:360). Thus, Ethiopians were considered to be Black people. In fact "Ethiopians were the yardstick by which antiquity measured colored peoples. The skin of the Ethiopian was black, in fact blacker, it was noted, than that of any other people" (Snowden 1970:2).

3. Snowden relies heavily on Diodorus for his information concerning the Ethiopians during Ptolemaic times. Snowden writes that "Diodorus cites three main sources for his description of Ethiopians—Agatharchides, Artemidorus, and interviews with Ethiopian ambassadors" (1970:109).

4. "House of women" (Breasted 1912:428).

5. Taharqa is definitely one of the most well known kings of antiquity. He is mentioned in the Bible in Isaiah 37:9. He was an ally with the people of Israel in a war against the Assyrians.

MATRIARCHY: EXAMINING THE EXALTED POSITION OF WOMEN IN KEMET AND KUSH

Cheikh Anta Diop in his book *The African Origin of Civilization: Myth or Reality* ([1955] 1974) postulates that the existence of matriarchy throughout Africa is one crucial piece of data that supports a Negro origin for ancient Egypt. He advances the theory that "the matriarchal system is the base of the social organization in Egypt and throughout Black Africa. In contrast, there has never been any proof of the existence of a paleo-Mediterranean matriarchy, supposedly exclusively White" ([1955] 1974).

Diop maintains that "matriarchy derives from the general idea that heredity is effective only matrilineally" (143). It is through motherhood that a "woman transmits political rights" (143). He proposes that the number and frequency of queens in Africa's political history is a result of matriarchy. Nevertheless, Diop cautions the reader not to "confuse matriarchy with the reign of the African

Amazons or that of the Gorgons. Those legendary regimes in which woman allegedly dominated man were characterized by a technique intended to debase the male" (145). Diop defines matriarchy in the specific sense of: *the tracing of the family through the mother and the transmission of political rights through the womb.*

In this chapter, past and current concepts of matriarchy in Africa will be surveyed for the purpose of determining whether matriarchy is a viable component of African culture. The Kushite culture will then be examined to determine if there is evidence of matriarchy in their cultural customs.

Diop's Two-Cradle Theory

Diop proposes that matriarchy is the key component differentiating cultures such as Greece from those of Africa. According to Diop, historian J. J. Bachofen was the first to develop an hypothesis concerning the prominence of matriarchy. Bachofen proposes a linear hierarchical analysis which places a lower social value on matriarchy than on patriarchy. Diop summarizes the premise put forth by Bachofen as follows:

> (Stage 1) Humankind, in its earliest state, passed through a stage of sexual wantonness, marriage did not exist, the only trustworthy method of tracing descent was matrilineally; (Stage 2) Marriage is practiced and matriarchy reigns; (Stage 3) Males become the dominant sex and patriarchy reigns; and (Stage 4) Patriarchy is superior to matriarchy. It "represents above all spirituality, light, reason and delicacy. It is represented by the sun, the heavenly heights, where reigns a sort of ethereal spirituality. In contrast matriarchy is linked with the cave-like depths of the earth, [with] the night, [with] the moon, [with] material things

> ...[with] passive femininity in opposition [with]...masculine activity. (5-6)

Bachofen's theory assumes that humans have progressed from matriarchy to patriarchy, in a kind of universal transition from darkness to light, the reign of women being symbolized by darkness and the reign of men by light. This is a classic case of Eurocentric thinking—the use of dichotomy; hierarchical ranking; the positive valorization of those characteristics that most parallel European culture; the demeaning of the place of women; and finally, the ascription of all of this to the universal proclivity of human beings. Diop offers an alternative theory which dispenses with Bachofen's "universal transition" and places matriarchy in a different light:

> [I]nstead of a universal transition from matriarchy to patriarchy, humanity has from the beginning been divided into two geographically distinct 'cradles' one of which was favorable to the flourishing of matriarchy and the other to that of patriarchy ...(Diop 1978, 19)

Diop suggests that three cradles of humanity functioned simultaneously: a northern zone, a southern zone, and a zone of confluence. The Nile Valley is included in the southern cradle. In the southern cradle, the female "becomes one of the stabilizing elements in her capacity as mistress of the house and keeper of the food; it also seems that she even played an important role in the discovery of agriculture and in plant selection, while man devoted himself to the hunt" (27-28).

This is unlike the northern cradle, in which the lifestyle is nomadic and "the economic role of the woman was reduced to an absolute minimum; she was merely a burden that the man dragged behind him. Outside her function of child-bearing, her role in nomadic society was nil" (23). The female, as a primary supporter of the family, has an eminent position in the southern cradle.

In Diop's two-cradle theory, the family traces its lineage through the mother. Descent is traced "from that married partner who does not leave the clan after marriage" (28). Therefore among sedentary peoples, descent will be matrilineal because the mother does not leave her clan; it is the husband who becomes part of her family (28).

Diop postulates that the key to understanding matriarchy is "the structure of the society which allows [the female] to play a leading economic role" (28-29). This factor cannot be stressed too strongly. In matriarchal systems, women have economic and political power and own property.

In the Nile Valley, males gained the political power of the throne through only marriage with females of royal birth. This practice had a two-fold purpose, "[i]n marrying their sisters, the pharaohs kept the throne in the same family and at the same time eliminated disputes about succession" (ibid., 53). This also had additional societal benefits, in that:

> the pharaoh who marries his sister is, at the same time, his son's uncle. Now, under the matrilineal regime, only the nephew inherits from his maternal uncle...In contrast, his own sons do not inherit from him and he, himself, does not belong to his wife's family. All these inconveniences are eliminated thanks to what has been called 'royal incest.' (53)

Diop argues that "African matriarchy existed on a continent-wide scale" (62). Matriarchy existed among the Ashanti of Ghana, the Bantu of Central Africa, Tswana of Bechuanaland in South Africa, and among other ethnic groups in Ghana and Mali before the arrival of Islam and Christianity (57-64). It was the arrival of external religions, Islam and Christianity, that brought the patrilineal system to Africa. Diop summarizes the position of women in Africa as follows: "The woman enjoyed a liberty equal to that of a man, had a legal individuality and could occupy any function (e.g., Candace, Queen of Ethiopia and commander of her army). She was already emancipated and no public act was alien to her" (127).

Diop's use of the word matriarchy has often been misunderstood. The etymology of matriarchy is '*arch*' meaning principal and '*matri*' meaning mother. Clearly in Africa, as in no European society, the role of the mother was principal or chief. In fact, Afrocentric advocate, Ifi Amadiume points out "At no period in the history of the patriarchal cultures of Europe has motherhood been accorded the same status and reverence it has had in African cultures" (Amadiume 1987 b, 3).

Yet matriarchy is most commonly used to denote a society in which women *rule*. In fact, *Webster's New World Dictionary: College Edition* defines matriarchy thusly: "1. a form of social organization in which the mother is recognized as the head of the family or tribe, descent and kinship being traced through the mother instead of the father. 2. government by women" (1968, 907). This edition of Webster's dictionary also defines matriarch as "a mother who rules her family or tribe" (907). This definition is based on an Eurocentric paradigm which is unable to discern complementary relationships from hierarchical ones. If a family traces its lineage through the mother and she has power, then the mother must rule. They can see only "either/or" divisions, not holistic patterns.

Diop is clear that the importance of women in Africa derives from their roles as mothers, providers of food and inheritors of property. In order to ascertain the position of women, the question becomes "whether this basic structure of mother and child is acknowledged in social organization, culture and politics" (Diop 1978, xv). The key component of matriarchy is not that the female rules, but that the female has a principal role in the culture. The male and female roles function together for the benefit of all.

Intellectual Foundations of Matriarchy

It is important for our purposes to survey matriarchy in the social anthropological literature, since it is a term that arose from the discipline of social anthropology—a discipline based on Europeans studying "the other." The concept of matriarchy arose from the kinship theories.

Anthropologist James George Frazer was one of the first scholars to examine matriarchy. In Part IV of *The Golden Bough*, he defines the concept as mother-kin. Frazer explicitly informs his readers that "mother-kin does not mean mother-rule" (Frazer 1961, 209). What it does mean is a "social system which traces descent and transmits property through the mother alone" (Book III, 202). The operative principle is the tracing of lineage and the transfer of property through the mother.

Frazer examines the practice of mother-kin under a monarchy. He illustrates how it functions by referring to Africa where "the chieftainship or kingship often descends in the female line, but it is men, not women, who inherit it" (Book III, 211). Frazer considers the ancient Egyptians as exemplars of how the system of mother-kin operated:

> In Egypt the archaic system of mother-kin, with its preference for women over men in matters of property and inheritance...was traditionally based on the example of Isis, who had avenged her husband's murder and had continued to reign after his decease. ...(III, 213-214)

Diodorus of Sicily was Frazer's source of information on this topic. Diodorus reports that:

> The Egyptians also made a law...permitting men to marry their sisters, this being due to the success attained by Isis in this respect; for she had married her brother Osiris, and upon his death, she both avenged the murder of her husband and reigned all her days over

the land with complete respect for the laws, and, in a word, became the cause of more and greater blessings to all men than any other. (Book I, 27, 85)

It is an historical fact that some Egyptian males of royal birth married their sisters. Does this mean that the ancient Egyptians practiced incest?

French anthropologist Claude Levi-Strauss posits that the prohibition of incest is a "universal concept," that is, a "criterion of nature, for what is constant in man falls necessarily beyond the scope of customs, techniques and institutions whereby his groups are differentiated and contrasted" (Levi-Strauss [1949] 1969). Levi-Strauss equates universal concepts with "the natural order." (8) The "incest prohibition" is a universal concept, in his opinion:

> [T]hat the prohibition of incest constitutes a rule need scarcely be shown. It is sufficient to recall that the prohibition of marriage between close relatives may vary in its field of application according to what each group defines as a close relative, but...this prohibition is nevertheless to be found in all social groups. (9)

Levi-Strauss cites the culture of Ancient Egypt as an exception to the rule. The actual historical Kemet, however, shoots several holes into his theory:

> Ancient Egypt is more disturbing since recent discoveries suggest that consanguineous marriage, particularly between brother and sister, was perhaps a custom which extended to the petty officials and artisans, and was not, as formerly believed, limited to the reigning caste and to the later dynasties. (9)

The marriage between sister and brother did keep the throne in the family and eliminated arguments about succession, as Diop has written. Additionally, as this writer has asserted, one must always analyze African culture from both the material and the spiritual levels. The ancient Egyptians believed that Aset and Asar were united in the womb, before birth, and they were *the* divine couple. This suggests that through marrying their siblings, in addition to assuring inheritance of the throne, the Kemites were reaffirming the divine order and upholding Maát.

Diodorus views the marriage of royal brothers and sisters in terms of power relationships:

> [I]t was ordained that the queen should have greater power and honour than the king and that among private persons the wife should enjoy authority over her husband, the husbands agreeing in the marriage contract that they will be obedient in all things to their wives. (Diodorus I, 27, 86-7)

This supposed authority of royal and nonroyal women over their husbands is a misinterpretation of African culture, a misinterpretation that is still evident today in Webster's definition of matriarchy. On the subject of women, the Greeks had difficulty understanding African culture because it was distinctly different from theirs.

In Greece, women could not own property. The position held by Grecian women can be demonstrated by the manner in which Aristotle viewed Spartan women:

> [T]he liberty permitted to Spartan women in the days of Sparta's great military successes had...led directly to her defeat by the Thebans. Women...lived intemperate and luxurious lives, while the men remained in military training...one particularly unfortunate consequence was that two-fifths of Sparta was owned by women...who *unlike*

their Athenian counterparts could inherit and bequeath property [emphasis added]. (Lefkowitz 1983, 55)

The women of Ptolemaic Egypt demonstrate the difference between women in Greece and those in Africa. Egyptologist Barbara Lesko informs us that during the Ptolemaic dynasty, there were two legal codes—one Greek, and one Egyptian:

> The Egyptian code continued to uphold the legal independence of a woman; and many Greek women resident in Ptolemaic Egypt chose to operate under Egyptian law rather than Greek, which gave them no such autonomy. (Lesko 1994-1995, 23)

Thus it becomes problematic to evaluate African culture based on interpretations by a Greek, as Frazer has done.

Matriarchy, essentially, is a system which is based on matrilineal descent which in turn can best be described as follows: "The individual's initial relationship is to his mother and through her to other kinsmen, both male and female, but continuing through females" (Schneider and Gough 1961, 3). The matrilineal system does require an active role of women for:

> female members must ensure that the children will achieve primary orientation to the matrilineal descent group and develop primary ties of loyalty to it. If males are required for authority roles then they, too, cannot be relinquished by or alienated from the group....(9)

Matrilineal descent also requires "the institutionalization of special limits on the authority of husbands over wives" (19). This differs from patrilineal descent groups which do not "require any other limits [on husbands] than those inherent in the problem of maintaining any system of social relations" (19). Thus, matrilineal descent does give certain rights to females that are not found in patrilineal societies, such as those of Europe.

The editors of the book *Matrilineal Kinship,* Schneider and Gough (1961), through the examination of primary source documents, surveyed several matrilineal societies. An examination of the Asante showed that royal succession was confirmed after the candidate had been "nominated by the Queen Mother after consultation with the stool family. The nomination not only had to be formally approved by the Kumasi 'elders' (i.e., the Asantehene's advisors, who were captains or lineage heads) but also by the Union chiefs of states" (277).

The close relationship between mother and child can also be seen in Asante culture.

> The crucial relationship in Ashanti kinship was that between mother and child....Moral rather than legal sanctions buttressed the mother's authority. She was seldom a punishing agent; rather, she stood for "unquestioning protection and support against the world at large." (291)

This close relationship between mother and child can also be an indication of a matri*focal* society. The term "matrifocal" is defined by Amadiume as "mother focused: a household arrangement around the mother and her children, the focal or reference point being the mother. Similarly, the matricentric unit is the mother and her children" (1987 b, 40).

In summary, the term matriarchy will be used hereafter to mean: descent traced through matrilineal kinship; a close relationship between mother and child; economic and political power of women.

Mothers of Kush

The revered position of the mother, common to African societies, is unquestionably manifested in Kushite culture.

The texts left by the Kushite kings contained many words of homage for their mothers. In addition to the texts, mothers were "always the first persons to be represented beside their sons in temple and other relief" (Macadam 1949, xi). In the stela of King Taharqa, Years 8-10, he not only illuminates the respect he has for the females in his family, he comments on his mother:

> (22) His Majesty did this he loved his father Amon-Re of Gematen so greatly....*on account of the miracle which he wrought for his mother in womb before she gave birth. For the mother of his mother was committed to him by her brother...the son of Re Alara* (23)

He speaks to the supreme deity about his sister:

> "O excellent god, swift of step, who comest to him that calls to thee, do thou look for me upon my sister, a woman born together with me in one womb. Do thou act for her even as thou act for him that acted for thee....Do thou for my sister in this wise; distinguish her children in this land; do thou grant that they attain prosperity and the appearing as king, even as thou hast done for me."

He then comments on how Re, his father, heard his petition to him, appointed him king and then bade him:

> to pronounce the names of his female ancestors, to establish funerary offerings for them, and to give them numerous *ka*-servants, rich in all things [emphasis added]. (Macadam 1949, VI 36)

In the stela of King Taharqa, Year 6, he explains how he was raised by his mother for twenty years, before he was selected as king. His mother and he played roles similar to Aset and Heru. As Aset nurtured and raised Heru to overcome his father's enemies and to become king, Abar appears to have raised Taharqa to become king. One can almost feel the respect and adoration that King Taharqa has for his mother. As Aset represented motherhood at its finest, Taharqa's mother was among humanity's finest. He expounds on her importance in this passage:

> [T]he King's Mother, Abar....found me crowned on the throne of Horus....And ...rejoiced exceeding...even as Isis saw her son Horus crowned upon the throne of his father after he had been as a youth within the nest of Chemmis. (20) Upper and Lower Egypt and every foreign country bowed to the ground before the Queen Mother....and acclaimed this Queen Mother (21) saying, 'Isis, when Horus had received her, was like the Queen Mother now that she has been reunited to her son...O mighty King, mayest thou live...even as Horus lived for mother Isis.' (V, 28)

King Anlamani ruled during the 2nd dynasty of Napata. This was contemporaneous with the 26th dynasty of Kemet. In Anlamani's stela, he also writes about his mother and the pride she had when he was crowned.

> Now the Queen Mother Nasala...the Mother of a King, pleasant of love, the mistress of all women, and His Majesty sent his courtiers (23) to fetch her. She found her son crowned like Horus upon his throne...even as Isis saw her son Horus crowned upon (24) earth. (Macadam 1949, VIII, 47)

Macadam, like Reisner, attempted to decipher family relationships of Kushite royalty. He laments that "The references to the 'mothers' of Taharqa's mother and the disclosure of the fact that these 'mothers' were sisters both of one another and of a king named Alara are sufficiently startling to warrant a re-examination of....Taharqa's genealogical tree" (xi). This is startling if one does not associate this culture with Africa. The role of mother and aunt and father and uncle is interchangeable in many African cultures, such as the Akan, Ashanti, and the Yoruba.

In the stela of King Taharqa, Year 6, he refers to "his mothers":

> (16) For he knew that his son, namely I, whom he begat, had made a monument for him [Amon-Re]. For the 'mother' of my mothers were committed to him (17) by their brother...the son of Re, Alara...
> (Macadam 1949, IV, 16)

The role of the mother in the lives of the common people of Kush is unknown to us. We do know that mothers had a venerated position among royalty. It would not be farfetched to posit that motherhood was very respected throughout the culture.

God's Wife Of Amun

The position of God's Wife of Amun was a very significant one for women in the Nile Valley. It is through this position that one can ascertain that females held far-reaching power in Kush. During the sixth dynasty of Kemet a queen named Neferu was the first to assume the title "Divine Wife of Amen" (Buttles 1908, 47). She was part of a dynasty associated with Thebes. Little else is known about this queen and the responsibility of this title. The next queen to hold the title was Aah-Hotep. She was a queen of the 17th dynasty and she held the title "Divine

Wife of Amun" and this title implied the "rank of chief high-priestess of Amen" (*ibid.*, 47).

The queen that brought the title to prominence was Ahmose Nefertari, the wife of the 18th dynasty king Ahmose. Queens had the right to use one name before their names, instead of the multiplicity of titles that customarily preceded it. They would usually choose the most meaningful title, such as "king's principal wife" or "king's mother." Ahmose Nefertari selected "god's wife" (Robins 1993, 44). Ahmose Nefertari appears to have established the format of the worship. Egyptologist Gay Robins writes that:

> A number of ritual offerings dedicated by Ahmose Nefertari have been found in temples....The evidence leaves no doubt as to Ahmose Nefertari's involvement....Much of this may have been in her capacity as god's wife, which Ahmose Nefertari seems to have regarded as equally as important as her position as queen. (Robins 1993, 44)

Ahmose Nefertari had a tremendous influence over Kemetic people and perhaps it was this influence that also extended to the title and position of God's Wife of Amun. Buttles informs us that:

> The worship of Nefertari which arose soon after her death, became a popular cult of a most unusual nature....Her devotees elevated her to the highest heavens, where, seated by Amun, Mut and Khonsu, she was adored as a divinity equal to the persons of the sacred Theban trinity....This worship of the queen and her family was more frequent and of longer duration than that of any other monarch....[T]his worship continued for some six hundred years after the queen's death. (Buttles 1908, 61)

Ahmose Nefertari's influence probably affected Hatshepsut. She was an 18th-dynasty queen. When Hatshepsut was married to Thotmose II, she assumed the role of queen. During this time, when she used one title before her name, the one that she preferred was "God's Wife" (Robins 1993, 46). Eventually, she rejected the insignia and role of queenship and declared herself "king of the north and south." She became one of the most powerful rulers of Kemet. When Hatshepsut became king she transferred the office of God's Wife to her daughter, Nefrure, who also used the title frequently as her only title (*ibid.*, 148).

No doubt, God's Wife of Amun was a pivotal office. By the 23rd dynasty, it appears that the title changed name and meaning. In the 27th Dynasty, the title "divine adoratrice" (*duat netjer*) became associated with the title "God's Wife of Amun" and the same women bore both (Robins 1993, 149). Egyptologist Barbara Waterson explains the change of the meaning in the title:

> [T]he title 'Divine Wife of Amun' was that of a daughter of the king who became the consecrated wife of the god, Amun....Being officially celibate and without children of her own, each 'Divine Wife of Amun' had to ensure the succession by adopting a 'daughter,' who was recognized as the heiress presumptive, and who, it has been suggested, bore the title 'Divine Voltaress.'
> (Waterson 1991, 160)

When Piankhi saved Thebes in 740 B.C.E., he installed his sister, Amenirdis I, as "Divine Wife Apparent." In this way, he established a solid power base. The female in this position "owned great estates....and employed a large number of officials to administer them. Because of their enormous wealth which enabled them to wield temporal power, and because of their religious position [whereby] they wielded spiritual power, they also enjoyed a considerable amount of political influence" (Waterson 1991, 160).

The power that the Divine Wife of Amun held can be gauged by a description of Karnak during the reign of Ramses III of the 20th Dynasty. There were 81,322 people in the service of the Amun, working under 125 categories. There were 421,262 animals, 433 gardens, and 83 ships. This was contained within 2,395 square kilometers of field, holding 46 work sites and 65 villages.[1] There is not as detailed a description of Karnak left during the 25th dynasty. However, the worship of Amun became more extensive and kings of the 25th Dynasty added to Karnak; thus we can safely assume that Karnak was considerably grander. The God's Wives of Amun wielded so much power that they were treated as queens and addressed as "Your Majesty" and their names were written inside of cartouches (160).

The Kandakes

> The line of Ethiopian queen mothers...may in turn have given rise to the Meroitic line Kandakes, and that the Meroitic *kdke* is simply the equivalent of *mwt nswt* 'King's Mother.'(Macadam 1949, xi-xii)

Women had enjoyed a longstanding tradition of respect and elevated position in Kushite culture. As previously stated, the position of God's Wife of Amun was a source of power over spiritual and material realms. Taharqa, Piankhi, and Anlamani all emphasize the importance of their mothers and wives in their coronation ceremonies and during their reigns. The appearance of a series of queen regents in Meroe, commonly called Candaces, can be viewed as a natural component of the elevated position of women in the Kushite culture. This could hardly have happened in Greece, where women neither owned property nor made decisions concerning the election of kings. This phenomenon is still not completely understood, partly because the Meroitic script is not understood and partly because some scholars do not understand the position of women in

African culture. William Adams (1977), for instance, emphasizes that:

> While Nubian society was by no means matriarchal, there can be no doubt that queens enjoyed an unusually high place as both *consorts and as dowagers*...It must have been the prestige and *behind-the-scenes power* enjoyed by the Nubian queens which gave rise to the Roman tradition that Kush was governed by a hereditary line of female rulers...[emphasis added].(260)

The very use of the concept "matriarchy" is confusing. Adams is not specific as to how he defines matriarchy. The cultural precedent in Kush which led to Candaces was not the dominance of women over men but reverence and high esteem for the abilities of women. We do not have much knowledge concerning the role of the common female in Kush, however royal women owned property and were rulers of Thebes. Adams' use of the terms 'dowager' and 'consort' suggests that these queens only owned property and gained power through their husbands, but in matrilineal kinship systems men obtain power through their marriage to women.

F. LL. Griffith (1916, III, 122) determined that the name Candace was a title and not a specific name. He almost singlehandedly deciphered the Meroitic alphabet, but the meaning of the words remains unknown. Reisner expresses the importance of Griffith's effort when he writes that "It has been Prof. Griffith's great service to human knowledge that he has determined the alphabetic character of both the Meroitic hieroglyphic writing and the cursive, has fixed the sound values of the letters of [these] two scripts and has made some progress in the translation of the texts" (Reisner 1922 V, 4, 175).

In the process of deciphering "The Great Stela of Prince Akinizaz," Griffith encounters a name that seems unusual to him. He comments that:

> *If the kingship in Ethiopia went by mother-right it would be strange that the queen should bear a non-native name....The queen's title...was read kzwe....we may accept this as the true reading....it is obvious that kazake is only another form of katake, Candace [emphasis added].* (Griffith 1917, 165)

In this passage, it is apparent that Griffith operated as if the kingship system were matrilineal and that the kingship was passed down through the mother. He used this assumption when he deciphered the name *katake* or Candace.

This is the name known to the ancient writers. Strabo informs us of one "Kandake" who was famous for her military valor. Strabo tells the story of how the Kandake attacked when the Roman force was distracted with fighting the Arabians in this manner:

> [T]he Aethiopians....attacked the Thebans and the garrison of the three cohorts at Syrene, and by an unexpected onset took Syrene and Elephantine and Philae, and enslaved the inhabitants, and also pulled down the statues of Caesar (Strabo 1982, XVII,i, 54, 139)

There is "a bronze head of the Roman Emperor Augustus (27 B.C.E. - 14 C.E.) found at Meroe" which is generally considered by scholars to have been taken during this attack (Hintze 1978, 101). This offensive attack demonstrates that these Africans were alert to opportunities to act in their own interest. This seems to go against Adams' argument that Meroe was primarily a reflection of classical European culture. The iconography and jewelry of Kush reflect cultural influences from the European classical world, yet the actions of *Kandake* against the Roman army reveals a people that considered themselves to be at least equal to the Romans. Strabo continues his narrative:

> But Petronius...first forced them to flee back to Pselchis, an Aethiopian city, and sent ambassadors...to ask *the reasons why they had begun the war; and when they said that they had been wronged by the Nomarchs,* he replied that these were not rulers of the country, but Caesar; and when they had requested three days for deliberation, but did nothing they should have done, he made an attack and forced them to flight, since they were badly marshalled and badly armed...[emphasis added]. (Strabo 1982, XVII, i,137-8)

The Africans attacked even though they were not as fully equipped as the Romans. They felt that they had been maltreated, so they waited until the Romans were vulnerable, then they struck. They were led in their attack by a woman and some of them were captured. Strabo reports:

> Among [the] fugitives were the generals of *Queen Candace, who was ruler of the Aethiopians in my time—a masculine woman, and blind in one eye.* These, one and all, he captured alive....After this he set out for Napata. This was the royal residence of Candace....But though she sent ambassadors to treat for friendship and offered to give back the captives and the statues brought from Syene, Petronious attacked and captured Napata too....(XVII, 139)

Strabo identifies the queen as Candace, as if that were her name. However, Pliny was aware that Meroe was ruled by "a woman, Candace, a name that has passed on through a succession of queens from years" (1989, VI, xxxv, 477). In Strabo's opinion she was a masculine-looking woman. She probably did appear different from the women of classical Europe.

The iconography generally shows the Kandakes to be large women with long, pointed fingernails and beautiful jewelry. Scholars have referred to these queens as large, fat, obese or very obese. Steffen Wenig maintains a position that "the amplitude of queens' figures is characteristic of later Meroitic....In contrast, the figures of goddesses are always slender" (Wenig 1978, 70).

St. Clair Drake offers the most lucid and comprehensive argument concerning the size of the *Kandakes*:

> Time as well as place is a factor in producing differences in aesthetic norms....For instance, a queen depicted as slaying enemies on a pylon of the Apedemek temple has "amplitude"...However, Queen Aminitore, when portrayed worshipping the Egyptian god, Amon, resembles the slender Egyptian type....These representations suggest that the context of action, and perhaps even age in the life cycle, may have determined how an artist portrayed a Meroitic female sovereign. (Drake 1991, 284)

The large size of the queen when depicted slaying enemies may indicate that the Kushites associated large size with power. Clearly, as Drake has noted, the difference in size had some cultural meaning for the Kushites. He continues:

> Some of the corpulent portrayals of the queens may be stylized representations symbolizing maternity and fertility, intended neither as realistic portraits of queens nor as the somatic norm image of women in the royal families. *What is significant is that the Meroitic queens had no objections to being represented as obese* [emphasis added]. (284)

There is a distinct possibility that the large size of the *kandakes* represented fertility and maternity. African culture must be viewed through the lens of spirituality. Fertility and motherhood have always had significance to African people. The *kandakes* were divine rulers. It is probable that they as women not only represented the fertility of the nation, as did male kings, but maternity as well because they were female. The *kandakes* were powerful women and in many African societies weight is symbolic of power.

Strabo acquaints us with the close relationship between the queen and her son. In fact, *kandake* means "queen mother." It is this relationship which may explain the role of Kandake as a ruler. It is believed by some scholars that some Kandakes were queen regents for their minor sons.

Strabo continues with a narrative that illustrates that this queen had considerable diplomatic skills as well as military prowess.

> Meantime Candace marched against the garrison with many thousands of men, but Petronious...bade them to go to Caesar; they asserted that they did not know who Caesar was or where they should have to go to find him, he gave them escorts....*And when the ambassadors had obtained everything they pled for, he even remitted the tributes which had imposed* [emphasis added]. (Strabo 1982, XXVII, 1, 141)

The Candaces were famous throughout the Roman world. Pliny also writes of the famous battle:

> Petronius captured the Arabian towns...*he also sacked the town of Napata*....Ethiopia was worn out by alternate periods of dominance and subjection in a series of wars with Egypt....[emphasis added]. (1989, VI, XXXV, 474-475)

The end result of this was that this Candace and her people lost the battle, but, through diplomacy, won the war. The Candace that was involved in this battle is believed to have been:

> either Amanirenas or her (immediate?) successor Amanishakheto....The two triumphal images of the pylon of [Amanishakheto's] pyramid chapel are predominately traditional illustrations of the ruler's role as victor over the country's enemies, and thus they cannot be interpreted as documentation of the conflict between Meroe and Rome. (Priese 1993, 12)

Fritz Hintze states that the "*kandake* against whom Petronious was compelled to fight is generally assumed to have been Queen Amanirenas" (1978, 100). He bases his presumptions on new inscriptions recently excavated at Qasr Ibrim concerning Prince Akinidad. The inscriptions "Akinidad together with Queen Amanishakheto, who was probably the successor of Amanirenas....[it] provides us with new evidence to prove that Prince Akinidad was intimately connected with Lower Nubia. He is the only person known to have borne simultaneously the two high titles of *paqor*, "prince," and *pesato*, "viceroy of (Lower Nubia)" (100).

Archeologist Paul Shinnie believes that the Kandake involved in this battle was Queen Amanishakheto because Queen Amanirenas is never mentioned without her husband, Netekamani (1967, 50). Shinnie declares that "Whatever the truth may be and whoever was the queen, Amanirenas or Amanishakhete...[she] so impressed the ancient world that the title of Candace became famous" (49). These contemporaries of the Meroites reported actions that contradict the image of consort or dowager or a force that operated "behind-the-scenes" that William Adams attributed to the Candaces (1977). This *Kandake*, acting in the interests of her own people, led a conflict that ultimately issued in peace between Meroe and Rome.

Kandake Amanishakheto

One of the most striking finds from antiquity is the treasure found in the pyramid of Kandake Amanishakheto. This researcher studied the treasures when they were exhibited at the Metropolitan Museum of Art in New York City on April 3, 1994. The exhibit was entitled "The Gold Of Meroe" and it was very impressive. Kandake Amanishakheto governed Meroe around 40-20 B.C.E. She was buried in a pyramid. There were more pyramids in Kush than in Kemet. On April 26, 1821, an indigenous African showed F. Cailliaud the pyramids. He became the first European to write about the ruins of Meroe.

> My guide told me that we would soon be able to see the [pyramids]. You can imagine the joy I felt when I caught sight of the tops of a host of pyramids, their tips majestically gilt by the rays of the sun, that had just lifted above the horizon!" (Priese 1993, 8)

These pyramids were different from those of Kemet in that they

> do not come to a point. Instead, they are capped by a level platform on which it is presumed there once stood a superstructure supporting a green or blue glazed ceramic slab in the form of a sun disk. (*ibid.*, 10)

Kandake Amanishakheto was buried in such a pyramid.

Giuseppe Ferlini was a military doctor in the Sudan in 1830. He left the military in order to excavate because he was "eager to make some useful contribution to history" (12). In actuality, as the following passage will reveal, he was, like others, primarily interested in robbing Africa of priceless treasures left by its ancestors. He destroyed several pyramids before he encountered the one that was eventually to bring him riches and place his name in history. Kandake Amanishakheto's lofty pyramid was about seventy feet at the base and was once well preserved. Ferlini destroyed it to the level of the roof (Griffith 1911, 77). The following passage discloses his racist tactics and purposeful attempts to conceal ancestral treasures from African people:

> Having climbed the pyramid, we found the servant lying on his stomach on the exposed surface, over an opening that had been uncovered. *The blacks wanted to drag the servant aside, so that they could reach down in the hole; with our guns we forced them to climb down....*
>
> I gathered up everything I found and packed it into leather satchels and in this manner hid the gold from the Arabs....as it became evening, and the blacks had returned to their huts, we brought the discovered objects to our tents...and I studied them with my soul filled with joy....[emphasis added]. (Priese 1992, 12-13)

Griffith, in his report of one of the first archeological excavations of Meroe, describes Kandake Amanishakheto, who is identified by her cartouche. She is depicted on the northern tower as

> very obese...holding four standing prisoners by a cord in her left hand, while the right pierces the neck of one with a javelin. (Griffith 1911, 77)

On the southern tower, she

> wears a tall headdress of disk and plumes, bundles, and ram's horns, with fillet and double uraeus round her head, and Ammon horns round her ears. She holds seven prisoners of various nations, together with a

bow and arrows, by a rope in one hand, and pierces one with a javelin. (77)

Kandake Amanitere

Kandake Amanitere is always associated with her husband Natak-Amani. Griffith noted that their names

> seem to be at least two...pairs, an earlier pair who affected Egyptian writing and Egyptian prenomens even in Meroitic writing, the other in the full Meroitic style. The names of both king and queen are compounded with that of Ammon. (Griffith 1911, 56)

The transformation of Meroitic script can be seen in their names. The prominence of Ammon can also be determined in their theomorphic names.

Griffith (1911) describes her as "an obese queen, with long nails as in all her representations here, wears a simpler diadem with the uraeus of Apezemak" (56). In Wad Benaga, which is near the bank of the Nile, he found her portrayed as

> [T]he queen with similar headdress, obese and with pendant breasts, clothed in a long garment to ankles, similarly supports the sky. Her Egyptian prenomen is over her left shoulder, "The Queen of Upper Egypt, Lady of the two lands, Mer-ke-re"; over the right shoulder her Meroitic name, "Daughter of the sun, Lady of diadems, Amanitere." (1911, 68)

She is equated with the celestial beings, and established as part of the divine order:

> Established art thou upon thy great place, O Isis, Lady of the Underworld, like as the

moon is established firm in the egg, circling round heaven: may she give life to the daughter of the Sun, Amanitere. (68)

Reisner determined that the "Second Meroitic Dynasty of Napata" was within the first century B.C.E. He noted that this Dynasty was unusual because "The first, the second and the fifth rulers were queens, while only the third and fourth were kings" (Reisner 1922, V, #4, 188)

Queen Nawidemak

Queen Nawidemak is not as well known as Amanishakheto or Amanirenas. She was a ruler and the mother of royalty. A depiction of her is shown on the pyramid known as Barkal 6 near the holy mountain, Jebel Barkal. He describes a depiction of her in this manner:

> She is seated on a couch in the conventional attitude of a deceased person....On each of the left and right walls of the chapel she appears in a shrine, wearing the clothes and holding the insignia which denote both her royalty and...her identity after death with the god Osiris....(Macadam 1966, 23, 2, 50)

It is interesting that even though she is a female, she is portrayed as a companion to Osar, the ruler of the underworld. Perhaps, this is because her position as a divine ruler is more important than her gender. Therefore, we find her

> accompanied by Isis, Osiris' consort, who stands on a lotus flower with wings outstretched around the queen in protective attitude. (Macadam 1966, 50)

This depiction gives us information about Nawidemak. Isis or Aset standing on a lotus with her wings outstretched is very significant. The lotus is a symbol of rebirth and "was also closely associated with the imagery of the funerary cult—the four sons of Horus....are sometimes shown on the flower which rises from a pool....before the throne of Osiris," and Chapter 81 of the Book of the Dead contains the spells for "transforming oneself into a lotus and thus into the reality of resurrection." (Wilkinson 1994, 121). Wings have been a symbol of protection in Kemet from at least the time of the Old Kingdom. Wilkinson writes that from very ancient times, the Egyptians conceived of the heavens as

> the wings of a great falcon....god Horus.... In the later periods the image of the winged sun disk occurs universally as a protective symbol above the entrance doors of temples and their inner rooms, and also along the central axis of the temple roof as a symbol of the daily procession of the sun....(101)

Queen Nawidemak is being protected by Aset as she is resurrected and becomes Osiris. Her royal status can also be determined by the insignia she has in her hand, the flail and her name written within a cartouche. Macadam writes that there is also a male figure, probably her eldest son or another heir, who holds in his hand a palm branch. Macadam believes that the palm branch represents Isis worship; however, like most symbols in African culture, it probably has a multiplicity of meanings. I believe, in this case, it may also represent Nawidemak's triumphant admission into timelessness. The palm branch was "the symbol of the god Heh...the personification of eternity... as a symbol of time, the palm branch is also found in...the illustrations of the second 'hour' of the Book of That Which Is in the Underworld...the figures of three gods appear...'The Opener of Time,' 'The Guardian of Time,' and 'The Carrier,' and show...the importance of the control of time for the deceased king's successful entry into eternity..." (Wilkinson 1992, 119). Thus, in many ways, Queen Nawidemak is being depicted as equal to a king.

There is additional evidence about Queen Nawidemak. She left an inscription, in Meroitic, which Macadam has interpreted as:

> O Ammon of Napata, I Nawidemak...the ruler, make presentation to the requiter of a benefit. (61)

Macadam also interpreted her name to mean "God hath Begotten" or "A god is born" (61). There is also a statue of her now in the Museum of Antiquities at Khartoum, which was reunited with a base that was at Oberlin College. She is not so large in this statue as she is depicted on the two-dimensional reliefs. Macadam suspects that "she was not yet a Candace when the statue was made, and that she is besides a little earlier than Amanitere" (69). At some point, she became a *kandake* and is one of the forgotten queens of *Africa*.

Summary

As stated by Diop, the matriarchal system was indeed the base of the social organization of Egypt and Kush. I have defined matriarchy in the context of African cultures. Matriarchy denotes that kinship was determined within a matrilineal system; women had political and economic power; and motherhood had an honored and revered position. Matriarchy does not imply rule of women over men, even though this is not precluded, as in the case of the kandakes. As has been stated, we do not know much about the common women of Kush, but, based on the cosmogony, the example of ruling women, and the respect for women's ability, we assume that they had a place of primacy in the culture also.

Women had power. Females passed down the legitimacy of kingship though their womb; prepared their sons for kingship; led battles; negotiated with rulers; conquered enemies; ruled the nation; and controlled large religious organizations. We can grasp the importance of their position when we see that their sons would not be coronated until their mothers arrived. Females in Kush can be credited with elevating a notable culture.

NOTES

1. This information was obtained during a visit the researcher made to Karnak. This is based on an inscription made during the reign of Ramses III.

CHAPTER SEVEN

TOTEMISM AND COSMOGONY: SURVEYING THE SACRED

☥

Diop (1955,1974) argues that it is important to examine totemism in Egypt because it "is absent from white populations" (135). Totemism is an essential element of ancient Egyptian culture. Moreover, it is found only in Black cultures (134). Totemism is therefore a cultural trait that Diop uses as evidence of an African origin for Ancient Egypt. In this chapter, arguments for and against the theory of totemism will be probed.

The role of cosmogony in African cultures will also be examined in this chapter. African cosmogony is brimming with images from nature. There is a synthesis of practice of the worship of deities and the infusion of nature. Diop asserts that "it cannot be denied that the Pharaoh participated in an animal essence (the falcon) just as we do today in Black Africa" (135).

Arguments in Support of the Existence of Totemism

Anthropologist James Frazer strongly supported and wrote extensively concerning totemism. He defines totemism as "a class of material objects which a savage regards with superstitious respect, believing that there exists and [sic] altogether special relation. The name is derived from an Ojibwa (Chippeway) word *totem*, the correct spelling of which is somewhat uncertain" (Frazer 1935, 1,3). The discipline of anthropology is replete with value-laden terms reflecting the Eurocentric perspective, such as "savage" and "superstitious." In order to use this definition, we must re-center terms. Totemism is the use of any material object or being that is perceived to be imbued with the living spirit (generally ancestral) and thus is deemed to be sacred and to warrant special deference, reference, and respect. Upon its consecration, the object becomes a living element to which one spiritually relates.[1]

Totemism as a Religion, or the Relation Between a Man and His Totem

Frazer asserts that totemism is based on mutually beneficial relationships. In these relationships:

> the totem protects the man, and the man shows his respect for the totem...by not killing it if it be an animal, and not cutting or gathering it if it be a plant....a totem is never an isolated individual, but ...generally a species of animals or of plants, more rarely a class of inanimate natural objects, very rarely a class of artificial objects. (3-4)

Frazer writes that "the members of [a] totemic clan call themselves by the name of the totem and commonly believe themselves to be actually descended from it" (5). Diop declares that currently in "Black Africa" some spouses have the same totemic names, such as N'Diaye, Diop, and Fall. These couples may not be aware that once it would have been taboo for them to marry each other. However, "[t]hey are clearly aware of being biologically parts of the very essence of the same totem. Both mates are quite conscious of sharing the same animal essence, the same biological essence; they are conscious of belonging originally to the same tribe, so much so that they often remind each other of that fact" (134-135).

Frazer supports his contentions with evidence of totemism from a myriad of ethnic groups. The examples are mostly from Native American groups, however he does devote sections to Africa. For example, he informs us that the Bechuanas in South Africa believe it is:

> ..."hateful and unlucky" to meet or gaze on a crocodile....So when a Crocodile clansman happens to go near a crocodile he spits on the ground as a preventive charm, and says, "There is sin." Yet they call the crocodile their father, celebrate it in their festivals, swear by it....(13)

Frazer does seek incidences of totemism in European culture. He believes that the lobster was considered a totem by the Greeks because they considered it sacred and did not eat it (15). He includes Europeans again when he describes that the purpose of totems is to not injure the faithful person, and to positively benefit him/her. He declares that "[m]embers of the Serpent clan in Senegambia profess to heal by their touch persons who have been bitten by serpents. A similar profession was made in antiquity by snake clans in Africa, Cyprus, and Italy" (22).

Frazer knows that he is on shaky ground in suggesting totemism in Indo-European cultures. He is irresolute when he writes that totemism may be regarded as certain for the Egyptians, and highly probable for the Semites, Greeks, and Latins. If proved for one Aryan people, it might be regarded as proved for all....(86-87)

Frazer's evidence is not conclusive either. He provides volumes of evidence of totemic practice among peoples of color but scant evidence for Indo-European people. Diop proclaims that "it is absent from white populations. Otherwise it would have been evident in the last white barbarian hordes who overran Europe in the fourth century. Those populations were at the ethnographic (clan, tribe) stage when totemism, if present, invests all acts of life and is evident at all levels of social organization" (1974, 134-135).

Social Aspect of Totemism, or the Relation of the People of a Totem to Each Other and to People of Other Totems

Frazer postulates that social relations arise from totemic practices. He posits that "all members of a totem regard each other as kinsmen or brothers and sisters, and are bound to help and protect each other. The totem bond is stronger than the bond of blood or family in the modern sense" (53). This bond extends to prohibitions against murder: because all members are assumed to be of the same essence, to kill a fellow totem member is analogous to killing god (54).

One of the chief elements of totemism is that marriage and/or sexual intercourse with a person of the same totem is very strictly forbidden. This is similar to incest taboos in that the clan severely punishes any one who breaks this rule.

One of the premises of the theory of totemism is that it is practiced during the beginning stages of the formation of every society. When societies advance (so the theory goes), totems transform into anthropomorphic gods. Also, there is a tendency to create a deity presiding over the totem species. Thus, Frazer sees totemism as the first stage of religion (82).

The Origin of Totemism

In Frazer's paradigm, totemism functions for the benefit of the ethnic group. This benefit was the primary reason for its development. He proposes that when the totem was beneficial to the group,

> ...it was the duty of the group to foster and multiply them; if, on the other hand, they were either noxious by nature...then it was the duty of the group to repress and counteract these harmful tendencies...and perhaps to turn them as efficient engines of destruction against foes. (116)

The reason for the prohibition against eating the totem, Frazer surmises, probably came from imitation of plants and animals, which do not feed upon their own kind (121).

The purpose of the totem, according to Frazer, is the "transference of a man's spirit or soul for safety to some external object....a totem is no more than a sort of strong box, in which a [person] keeps his soul....it is possible that the other motive—the natural desire of frail man to put all that is mortal of him beyond the reach of chance and change—may also have operated" (129). The totem, in this sense, becomes the embodiment of the spiritual forces for the whole group. If Frazer's premise is true, then we again meet with the importance of spirituality to African people.

Another argument for the existence of totemism was presented by Alexander Moret and G. Davy in *From Tribe To Empire: Social Organization among Primitives and in the Ancient East* (1926). They theorize that the first grouping of humans was not based on spatial proximity. These first groups were not involved in agriculture, nor were they sedentary. The cohesion was not based on blood kinship.

What held humans together was religion. Moret and Davy maintain that "[t]he original constitutional right is mystic in nature. It further may be shared in all the ways which are characteristic of mystic thought itself" (11). Moret and Davy explain the method in which the totem trusses the clan:

> [i]ts cohesion arises from the fact that its members regard themselves as bearers of one common totem and consequently one common name, made of one common mystic substance—that of their totem (12).

The members of the clan believe that they have a common origin, but it is not based on consanguinity. Kinship is "based simply and solely on community of totem" (13). In this system, spirit is thicker than blood.

There are certain duties which come with membership in the clan. These duties include: "avenging injuries done to a member of the clan...joining in its worship ...marrying outside of the clan (exogamy and, from the point of view of the family properly so called, prohibition of incest), and...abstaining from eating the animal serving as totem" (14). The totemic clan functions similar to a family. The principal difference is that the family is a consanguineous group. It is a "narrower, specialized, hierarchical group, in which the feudal type of sovereignty obtains, a type consequently more artificial than the diffuse sovereignty of the clan" (14).

Totemic society is equalitarian. There is no truly centralized political authority. Moret and Davy declare that "participation in the same totem, which constitutes the essence of each and cohesion of all, places all members of the clan on the same footing" (14-15).

Totemism as a Religious System

Blood is the essential element in totemism as a religious system. Moret and Davy expound on this concept:

> Now, totemism is a religious system which implies a whole universe of ritual prohibitions or taboos of which exogamy is one manifestation. *We know that the members of the clan are in a relation of mystic consubstantiality with the totem. Its essence is also theirs*....this essence...resides more particularly, in certain privileged parts of the organism and, above all, in the blood [emphasis added]. (17-18)

Again, like Frazer, Moret and Davy posit that the members of the same totem clan are all of the same substance. Blood contains the essence. Herein may lie the centrality of the female to the group:

> the...woman's blood in the system of uterine kinship...transmits the totem to her children. On the other hand, *the physiological constitution of woman brings about that by periodically losing blood she allows the sacred principle which she contains to escape and exposes it to the dangers of contact*. It can be understood, then, that contact with woman should be absolutely prohibited.... the prohibition applies only to individuals who belong to the totem. [emphasis added]. (18)

Residues of this system may explain the prohibitions against touching menstruating women by weavers of kente. There are some unwritten rules concerning the weaving of kente. Women are not allowed to be weavers because their menstrual periods are considered to interfere with the production of cloth or their menstrual periods may cause negative developments around the finished cloth. This may be based on the concept that when a women menstruates, she is allowing the sacred principle to escape and this may be in a manner that cannot be controlled.

Totemism in Ancient Egypt

Moret and Davy propose that "the true totemic society....knows neither kings nor subjects" (5). Ancient Egypt was a society that was based on a monarchy that lasted for at least 4,000 years. It was not, by this definition, a totemic society; Moret and Davy, however, propose that it had vestiges of totemism. Totemism was found "within a single personality—that of the king" (4). The basis of the totemic belief was that the king, the gods, and the people were of the same essence (8). The Kemites called this common essence the *ka*. Moret and Davy describe the *ka* as that which:

> animates at once the matter in inanimate bodies, the flesh of animate beings, and the faculties of the spirit....this genius which they called the *ka* (a word which, like *genius* itself, means generative force and protecting spirit) played the role of common substance and collective soul. (8)

The name taken by the king during coronation gives evidence of how significant the *ka* was to Kemites. The "ka and the totem-falcon were embodied in the sole person of the king to form his divine Horus name, it is probable that in the primitive period the *ka*, like the totem belonged to everyone, and not to individuals only but also to things" (8). For example Maát-Ka-Re was the Horus name assumed by Hatshepsut when she crowned herself Pharaoh. It means that Maát contains the same essence as the sun. In Moret's paradigm this would be considered a vestige of totemism.

To understand the manner in which Moret and Davy postulate that totemism functioned in Kemetic culture, we must once again turn to divine kingship. The ancient texts are replete with references to the falcon nature of the king:

> The first is the name of the falcon Horus... that means that the king is the falcon incarnate. In the classical period....A royal prince is called as a baby "the falcon in his nest." When he ascends the throne he is "the falcon on his palace." If the king die [sic] he is the "falcon winging his way to heaven" to return to the bosom of the god whence he is sprung. (140)

Thus Moret and Davy argue that dynastic Egypt used the totem in a more progressive way than did clans. In an Afrocentric world-view, however, cultures are not progressing to the supremacy of "civilization." The Kemites used the essence of the falcon in a manner that was beneficial to them at the time. It was embodied in the king who represented all of the people. Moret and Davy declare that "there is nothing abstract about this symbol; it conserves all its original realism" (140). In African culture, the unseen is real. The essence of the falcon was as real as the king. The falcon goes into battle:

> ...borne upon a shield going before the king....He fights for the kings, seizes his foes, and brings them captive to him. To write the name of King Aha (Menes)...the sculptors of Negadah depict the javelin and targe as clutched in the talons of the falcon. (140)

In addition to the falcon, the king assumed the characteristics of other totems. "One of the predecessors of Menes revered a scorpion as patron. The insect not only gave his name to this King Scorpion, but entered the battlefield as his champion...Another of his predecessors, Narmer, took as his name and represented on earth the fish *Nar*; it, too, comes to life to brandish a mace with both hands over the head of a defeated Asiatic" (142). Menes and other Old Kingdom Pharaohs assumed the quintessence of the lily of the South, the bee of the North, the vulture of Nekheb, and the uraeus of Buto, which all became part of the royal insignia.

Moret and Davy acknowledge that the majority of Egyptologists argue against the existence of totemic practices in dynastic Egypt. The main argument they advance is that endogamy, not exogamy, was practiced by them, because royal brothers and sisters married each other. They explained the social role played by guardian animals as zoolatry (144). Moret and Davy profess not to take sides in the argument; however they note that it is common historical practice for kings to assume characteristics once held by all the people. They also note that the arguments against the existence of totemic practices in Kemet do not seem decisive (144).

Totemism is assumed by Moret and Davy to be the concept that would best express the role played by the Falcon Horus to the first Pharaohs.

> Where the system of totemic clans exists, the totem (animal or otherwise) gives its name to the territory occupied by the clan; in Egypt a Falcon nome existed, and later on the whole of Egypt was called "the eye of Horus," a mystic name which, being interpreted, means "the creation of the Falcon." The men of the clan and its chief bear the totem's name; so do the followers of Horus and the Pharaoh Horus in relation to the falcon totem. (143)

This similarity continues in the place of worship for, in totemic societies, when the totem is placed in the shrine, it ensures protection, good fortune and food to the group. Likewise in ancient Egypt, the Falcon was considered to make her victorious and to provide her with gifts (143).

In battle, we see the use of the totem as a source of spiritual power. Therefore we find that:

> ...the Falcon's ensign goes before in the martial scenes depicted on palettes and mace-heads...Have we not seen the Falcon wielding targe and lance and leading prisoners taken in battle with a rope? (143)

One of the premises of totemic theory is that at various times the totem has intercourse with the chief's wife. The totem becomes the spiritual ancestor through this process. The concept of divine kingship posits that:

> ...the king of Egypt is the offspring of the union of the queen with the tutelary god of the Dynasty, who in this office has taken the Falcon's place. It looks, then, as if *the primitive Egyptian king stood in the same relation to the Falcon as the chief of a totemic clan to his totem* [emphasis added]. (144)

Arguments Against Totemism

French social anthropologist Claude Levi-Strauss presents the most decisive argument against the theory of totemism and in the process reviews some of the arguments of the advocates of totemism. He begins his argument in *Totemism* ([1962] 1969) with hesitation, for "to accept as a theme for discussion a category that one believes to be false always entails the risk, simply by the attention that is paid to it, of entertaining some illusion about its reality" (84).

Levi-Strauss first clarifies what is meant by the term *totem*, which, he declares, "covers relations, posed ideologically, between two series, one *natural*, the other *cultural*. The natural series comprises on the one hand *categories*, on the other hand *particulars*; the cultural series comprises *groups* and *persons* "(84).

Levi-Strauss has termed "the totemic illusion" that which is the result of semantic distortions and misinterpretations of cultural components. He asserts that "[c]ertain aspects of this field have been singled out at the expense of others, giving them an originality and a strangeness which they do not really possess; for they are made to appear mysterious by the very fact of abstracting them from the system of which, as transformations, they formed an integral part" (86).

Levi-Strauss uses the Ojibwa, a native American ethnic group, from which the word *totem* originates, to provide evidence of the distortions. He declares that "[r]esearches on the Ojibwa show that the first description of the supposed institution of 'totemism'—due to the English trader and interpreter, Long, at the end of the eighteenth century—resulted from *a confusion between clan-names* (in which the names of animals correspond to collective appellations) *and beliefs concerning guardian spirits* (which are individual protectors) [emphasis added] (87).

Levi-Strauss declares that totemism becomes problematic because, in order to use it, one must dichotomize cultures. The way that the theory is constructed, it does not allow one to view cultural components as parts of a whole system.

The totemic illusion establishes opposition, for instance, between personal relations and collective relations (88). For example, the totemic relationship is distinguished as different from that of the guardian spirit. It discourages construction of holistic systems; rather it encourages "uniting one group of men to one animal species....in such a fashion that a plurality of groups, on [the] one hand, and a plurality of groups on the other, are placed directly in correlation and in opposition" (88).

In a chapter called "Australian Nominalism," Levi-Strauss dialogues with a supporter of totemism, A.P. Elkin, who asserts that there are various types of Australian "totemism." Elkin maintains the concept of totemism even though, in order to conserve it, he found it necessary to divide it into: individual, social, cult, dream, and totemism divided by sex, moiety[2], section, sub-section and clan (113). Levi-Strauss argues that "there is no link to be seen between Elkin's rich and penetrating inquiries and this summary synthesis. The gap between the two levels recalls irresistibly that which...certain people criticized Gretry's harmony, saying that between his high notes and his low you could drive a carriage" (125).

Levi-Strauss also examines E. Durkheim's argument in support of totemism. Durkheim believes that one should treat one society at a time and rejects psychology as an anthropological explanation. Durkheim views "totemic codes as communications" and Levi-Strauss agrees with this premise. To the question "Why does totemism call on animals or plants?" (130), Durkheim replies:

> the permanence and continuity of the clan require only...an arbitrary sign....If it is later 'recognized' that these signs represent animals or plants, this is because animals and plants are present, accessible and easy to signify (130)

Levi-Strauss then reframes the question to ask, "Why do the majority of what are called primitive peoples adopt in their custom and myth a ritual attitude towards animals and other species?" (131). Radcliff-Brown answers that question as follows:

> If totemism chose natural species to serve as social emblems for segments of the society, this is quite simply because *these species were already objects of ritual attitudes before totemism* [emphasis added]. (131)

This is the reverse of the explanation given by Durkheim, who asserts that "totems are objects of ritual attitudes ['sacred' in Durkheim's terminology] because they were first called upon to serve as social emblems" (132).

Radcliff-Brown repudiates Durkheim's argument by saying that it is a result of a partial understanding of the sacred. However, to say that the totem is sacred is also not a good argument, according to Levi-Strauss, because ritual relation is "a collection of attitudes and obligatory ways of behaving. Consequently, the notion of the sacred does not supply an explanation: it merely refers the issue to the general problem of ritual relations" (130).

Levi-Strauss argues that Durkheim's theory relies too much on affectivity. Durkheim believes that "the existence of totems results from the recognition of animal or plant effigies in what were previously only non-figurative and arbitrary signs" (141). Durkheim's theory rests on a "*petitio principii*: it is not present emotions, felt at gatherings and ceremonies, which engender or perpetuate the rites, but ritual activity which arouse the emotions" (142). Levi-Strauss declares that "impulses and emotions explain nothing: they are always *results*, either of the power of the body or of the impotence of the mind. In both cases they are consequences, never causes" (142).

Totemism as a formally defined concept began with the American anthropologist, Boas. It is an artificial concept such as myth. Myth is used "arbitrarily in order to bring together under one word attempts to explain natural phenomena, products of oral literature, philosophical speculations, and cases where linguistic processes emerged to full consciousness" (79). It provides a framework under which to organize information. Totemism functions in a comparable manner. Levi-Strauss maintains that "totemism is an artificial unity, existing solely in the mind of the anthropologist, to which nothing specifically corresponds in reality" (79).

The concept becomes problematic because once it is posited, cultural components are then manipulated to fit into the paradigm. The champions of totemism typically misconstrue two concepts, according to Levi-Strauss:

> The first problem is that posed by the frequent identification of human beings with plants or animals, and which has to do with very general views of the relations between man and nature, relations which concern art and magic as much as society and religion. (79)

This is clearly a phenomenon that is most prevalent in African and Native American cultures. Social groups identify with plants and animals and associate the relationship between themselves and plants and animals with rituals and other spiritual activities. The second phenomenon that anthropologists examine is:

> the designation of groups based on kinship, which may be done with the aid of animal or vegetable terms but also in many other ways. (79)

This is used to explain exogamy. As Levi-Strauss points out, Boas' theses suggest a social system. The system uses animal and vegetable names as a mode of differentiation (81). However, this poses a different question, which is, "why the plant and animal domains should offer a specially favorable nomenclature for denoting a social system, and what relations exist logically between the system of denotation and the system that is denoted" (81). Levi-Strauss suggests that the animal world and plant life are used because they suggest "a mode of thought" (81). To postulate a connection between the "relation of man to nature and the characterization of social groups" can only be made real through the indirect mode of "passing through the mind" (81).

Levi-Strauss believes the ultimate goal of those who support totemism is "to strengthen the case of those who tried to separate primitive institutions from their own" (176). He believes that it is basically an illusion.

This researcher finds it necessary to modify Diop's use of the term totemism as an indicator of African culture. The term totemism has been defined in many ways, as the previous section demonstrates. However, there seems to be basic agreement that the term involves:

> 1. The association of human beings with plants, animals, minerals or stones. This association usually involves cosmological issues. 2. the systematic arrangement of

kinship based on identification with the plant, animal, stone or mineral.

Totemism has become an all-embracing concept that is used to explain various activities. The theory has become such an all-embracing concept that anthropologists have perhaps been blinded by the shine of the concept, and have failed to see what was really happening in cultures. For the purposes of analyzing the culture of Kush, the term totemism will not be used. There is a definite relationship between groups of humans and nature, that occurs most frequently among African and other groups that do not have Indo-European ancestry. This relationship has mystic attributes that cannot be explained through scientific modes of thought. These are factors that are keys to unlocking African cultural commonalities.

The primary component of so-called totemism is that the social groups believe they and the plant, animal, stone, or mineral are made of the same essential elements. They therefore choose not to kill or eat it. John Mbiti explicates this "premise of common essence:"

> African people have many religious associations with [plants and animals], some of them are linked with concepts of God. There are myths which tell how domestic animals originated at the same time or in the same way as man himself...the Zulu narrate that both men and cattle sprang from the same spot....The Akamba hold that cattle, sheep and goats accompanied the first human being whom God lowered from the sky. (Mbiti 1990, 50)

There is clearly a relationship between African people and nature that is different from the relationship between Indo-Europeans and nature. Totemism will be defined as a spiritualized object or being which is deemed sacred and warrants special deference, reverence, and respect. The spiritualized object becomes a living element to which one spiritually relates. The role of the totem in marriage will not be a part of the operational definition. This is part of the definition of totemism that cannot be asserted as a definite aspect of African culture. The more pertinent issue is that there are numerous examples which demonstrate that African people live in accordance with nature. They and nature are of the same *essence*, and function together. The dictionary defines *essential* as "that which constitutes the absolute essence or the fundamental nature of a thing and therefore must be present for the thing to exist" (Webster 1968, 496). African people simply recognize the common essence between themselves and what Europeans call Nature.

Wade Nobles describes this as the ontological principle of consubstantiation. He asserts that "To the Ancients, all the elements of the universe were 'consubstantial.' That is to say, the nature of all things was of the same spirit or *Ka*...all things are endowed with the spirit of God, (i.e., the *Ka* of God)" (1986, 107). This principle of consubstantiation allows us also to relate the relationship of totemism to cosmogony. African cosmogony is replete with use of animals, plants, stones, and/or minerals as spiritual objects. In order to explore cosmogony, we must include the concept of the common essence between humans and nature.

Cosmogony

Diop asserts that "Negro cosmogonies, African and Egyptian, resemble each other so closely that they are often complementary. To understand certain Egyptian concepts, one must refer to the Black world, as attested by what we have said about kingship" ([1955] 1974, 139). Diop defines cosmogony as "mores, customs, traditions, and thinking" (139). The similarity of these concepts is so strong that "it would take a lifetime to report all the analogies between Egypt and the Black world" (139).

Diop cites Paul Masson-Oursel's discussion of the Negro character of Egyptian philosophy to point out "what should be a cliche—the African aspect of the Egyptian mind—we can use...to account for more than one of its cultural traits" (139). The common mental structure of African people should "be obvious to anyone of good faith" (140).

Muntu (1961) by Janheinz Jahn, which postulates that there is a common mode of thinking among African people, provides a useful framework for discussing the similarities of African philosophies. Jahn examined the works of five different authors who had examined five different ethnic groups of African descent—Baluba, Ruandese, Dogon, Bambara and Haitians—which were found to all basically agree with each other (99).

The basic premises of African philosophy were postulated by Alexis Kagame, a Bantu, who wrote—and later published—his dissertation on Bantu philosophy. Janheinz Jahn based his book *Muntu* on Kagame's work and simplified Kagame's classification into four basic concepts, as follows:

1. *Muntu* = 'human beings' or intelligent being
2. *Kintu* = 'thing' or non-intelligent being
3. *Hantu* = 'place and time'
4. *Kuntu* = 'modality'(Jahn 1989, 100)

The common factor among these forces is *Ntu*. It is the cosmic universal force that is never separated from its manifestations, *muntu, kintu, hantu,* and *kuntu* (101). These forces are interconnected and complementary. There is rhythm in the forces. The forces operate in an harmonious and structured fashion. This is different from the structure of European culture. This can be demonstrated in the African concept of the Supreme Being. Jahn asserts that:

> God might be banished from Greek thought without any harm being done to the logical architecture of it, but this cannot be done in the case of the Yoruba. In modern times, God even has no place in scientific thinking. This was impossible to the Yorubas since from the Olodumare[3], an architectonic of

> knowledge was built in which the finger of God is manifest in the most rudimentary elements of nature. (97)

This is not only true for the Yorubas, but for ethnic groups throughout Africa. Spirituality is so woven into the tapestry of African culture that to separate it would unravel the whole cloth.

Ntu, the universal force, is "a central point at which living and dead, real and imaginary, past and future, communicable and incommunicable, high and low, are no longer conceived of as contradictory " (101). Everything in the universe is a force and *muntu* is the force under which humans are categorized. The category of *muntu*, human-beingness, also includes the dead, the *orishas*, the *loas*, and other deities. It is the force that has control over Nommo, "the word, and water and seed and blood in one" (101).

Muntu does have a visible body, but the human body is not *muntu*. Jahn declares that:

> When a man dies, therefore, his biological life (buzima) is in fact over, and his spiritual life (magara) also ceases—but something remains, namely that 'life force' Nommo which formed his 'personality'—what Temples calls the 'genuine' Muntu." *Manzima*, a living human being, becomes *muzimu*, a 'human being without life.' (107)

The ancient Egyptians must have believed that the deceased had a powerful life force. They wrote letters to ancestors. Kemites and Kushites built pyramids so that they could house the spirits of divine kings and queens and in turn receive benefits from their *ka* after death. To the people of the Nile Valley, the life force of the *muntu* was not terminated by physical death.

According to Jahn's interpretation, the concept of *muntu* is that which causes activity in the world. He asserts that:

> Only through the effect of a muntu, a man, living or dead—and that includes the ancestors, the orishas and even God—can 'things' become active and in their [activity] influence other 'things' and also rational creatures....(121)

Muntu, humanbeingness, is able to cause activity because it possesses "active intelligence" (121). This is the only one of the four basic concepts of African philosophy to have active intelligence or *ubwenge*. Animals have only memory. They are passive receptors, even though they also have five senses. This active intelligence, *ubwenge*, increases as one lives longer and gains experiences which lead to wisdom. Hence, in African culture, there is a tremendous respect for the elders who not only have increased *ubwenge* (wisdom) but are closer to the ancestors.

It is through *nommo* that *muntu* gains power over *kintu* (things). The generative power of the word, *nommo*, is with the *muntu*. This is evident in what is known as African sculpture. The metal, wood, stone, or clay from which the artist makes a work of art is only a *kintu*, a thing. The Eurocentric perspective views the African as worshipping the thing, the so-called "idol." However, the respect is never for the thing but for the *muntu* who have chosen to locate themselves there. The *kintu* becomes a spiritualized object, a "totem." The *muntu* gives the carvings meaning through *nommo*. In Kush and Kemet, carvings of deities were assumed to be the deities. They are totems. It was the *muntu*, in the role of priests using *nommo*, who gave them power. The *muntu*, the deities, were perceived to be residing within them.

In some African ethnic groups, the *muntu* who were dead had power over the living. According to Robert Farris Thompson in *African Art in Motion* (1974), the chiefs of the Kongo derived their power through the deceased. Thus, the staff was a symbol of the ancestors' power. When the chief had to make important decisions, "[he] might place his staff at the head of his bed.....hoping that the ancestors might reveal, in dreams, the true tradition, to teach him what to say on the following day" (63).

Totemism in Kush

In order to examine totemism in Kushite culture one must examine cosmogony. The concatenation of the relationship of Kushite people to animals, plants, stones, and minerals and their relationship to spiritual forces, philosophy, and modes of thinking are all part of the rich tapestry of African culture.

There are as many examples of links as there are deities. Diop gives an example of the similarity between the Dogon God-serpent and the God-serpent of the Egyptian Pantheon (140). The following section will focus on an examination of Amun. It will be shown that through the worship of Amun, Kemite and Kushite cultures were linked. The relationship between spiritualized objects, totems, and cosmogony—that is, mores, customs, traditions, and thinking—will also be illustrated in this section.

Amun

According to the Pyramid Texts (e.g., Unas, line 558), Amun is mentioned as one of the primeval gods. He is placed after the deities of primeval matter, Nau and Nen, and immediately before Shu and Tefnut. This is an indication that the ancient Egyptians "assigned great antiquity" to his existence (Budge 1904, II, 2). His name means "hidden" and he "was the personification of the hidden and unknown creative power which was associated with the primeval abyss gods in the creation of the world and all that is in it" (2). This indicates he was "the god who cannot be seen with mortal eyes, and who is invisible, as well as inscrutable, to gods as well as men" (2).

Up to the time of the 12th Dynasty, Amen was a local god of Thebes. However, when Thebes became the capital of Kemet, his importance rose. Budge reports that "the priests of Amen succeeded in making their god, both theologically and politically, the greatest of the gods in the country" (4).

His power increased when, in addition to his immense influence, he assumed the attributes of Ra. Budge reports that:

> The highest conception of Amen-Ra under the XIXth and XXth Dynasties was that of an invisible creative power which was the source of all life in heaven, and on the earth, and the great deep, and in the Underworld, and which made itself manifest under the form of Ra. (5)

The Color Blue

All aspects of African culture can be viewed through both a material and a spiritual lens. In this section, we will see that the color blue can be used to determine the position of Amun and Maát in the cosmogony of Kemet and Kush. Amun has been associated with the color blue. His original color was reddish-brown (similar to the color the people of Kush used to represent themselves), or sometimes black. However, from the post-Amarna period onwards, he is portrayed as blue. After Akhenaten's demise, the ancient gods were restored to their place in the pantheon. Amun was placed at the head. It is surmised that Amun was portrayed as blue in order to emphasize his position as the king of the gods (Dolinska, 1990, 5).

The color blue, then as now, was associated with the sky, and Amun was a sky god. However, the color blue also had other spiritual significance to the ancient Egyptians:

> [T]he color blue—the color of sky, of water, often a color of fertility (like green and black), and also the color of lapis lazuli... [was] valued more than any material except gold. Lapis lazuli belongs to divine things, the eyes, wigs, and beards of gods were made of this stone. (6)

We can gauge the importance of Amun from the color in which he is depicted. The change of Amun from reddish-brown to blue appears to be related to his elevation in the pantheon of the gods. Maát was associated with Amun through the color blue. Maát was an integral part of the culture of the Nile Valley. Maát had many attributes and influenced the culture of Kemet and Kush on many levels. One of them was as a goddess who "was in charge of maintaining equilibrium in the world" (Manniche 1994-1995, 59). She performed this task though the assistance of the divine ruler. Maát was associated with the creation story. She was represented by an ostrich feather which is "*niwu*" in hieroglyphics (a play on words, as "*niwu*" is also a word for creation). She was so important that even the gods had to obey Maát (Lecture by Theophile Obenga, April 5, 1995, Temple University). Another indication of the significance of Maát was that Akhenaten maintained Maát. Manniche reports that:

> even in the heretic Amarna period, Akhenaten himself is shown offering a figurine of the goddess to Aten. Perhaps it is Maát…who best reflected the significance of women in pharaonic Egypt. Without them social stability and even the continuation of humanity would have ceased. (ibid., 59)

The color used to write *maát* (Gardiner [1927] 1994, Aa, 11, 541) was changed to blue. Dolinska speculates that "[p]erhaps this was done to emphasize the connection between Maát, the divine order and harmony of the world, and Amun, king of the gods" (6). In using the color blue to write *maát* and *Amun* the ancients appear to be conveying the significance of Amun to the divine order and subsequently to divine kingship.

Amun as a Ram-God

Amun was a ram-god, similar to Hersyshef, Khnum, and the Ram of Mendes. One of the differences between Amun and the other three was the type of ram which was used to represent them.

> While the rams of the last three belong to the original breed in Egypt, *Ovis longpipes palaeoaegypticus*, that of Amun is different, being *Ovis platyura aegyptiaca*. During the Old Kingdom the flocks of sheep were composed of the one breed only, *longpipes*, but those of the Twelfth Dynasty and later include also the new importation, *platyura*. (Wainwright 1934, 141)

Ovis longpipes is identified "by its heavy build and long, horizontally undulating horns...the funerary papyrus of Khonsurenep. This long-coated ram is drawn....standing on a plinth which bears the feather of truth" (Wilkinson 1994, 61). Rarely is the solar deity represented as *ovis longpipes* in full form, but rather as "the head alone within the sun disk or as a ram-headed man, falcon or scarab, all these variants representing the sun in the evening and nightly aspects of its daily cycle" (61). The solar ram could also be associated with Osar and "in the Middle Kingdom the ram of Mendes was specially called the *ba* or soul of that god—perhaps as a play on the animal's onomatopoeic name" (61).

The ram which represents Amun, the *Ovis Platyura*, is "depicted with its down-curved horns and slighter build [than *longpipes*]" (61). Most of the time the ram of Amun is depicted prone and "it is [in] this pose that the god is depicted in the valleys of ram-headed crynosphinxes at Karnak and Luxor" (61).

It has been suggested that the rapid infusion of ancient Egyptian culture into Kush was a one-way route, from Kemet to Kush (Reisner 1923; Adams 1977). The acceptance of Amun as a national god has been thought of as occurring through force when Kemet occupied Nubia; or because the people of Nubia, in general, had no known religion before being occupied by the ancient Egyptians. Quite to the contrary, archeologist Bruce Williams asserts, "elements of the tradition often either combined with, were supplanted by, or even replaced, Egyptian motifs in a way that indicates considerable *reciprocity* existed in the relationship between Egypt and countries to the south" (Williams 1991, 74). This reciprocity is usually recognized at the level of the rulers, but there is also evidence of it at other levels of the culture:

> In addition to the formal culture of the rulers, Egyptian customs appeared in C-Group, Pan Grave, and Kerma cemeteries earlier, were used coherently, but did not efface local customs until the early New Kingdom. On the other hand, some practices typical of Nubia occurred in early Middle Kingdom Egypt.(84)

Williams further maintains that:

> *the mixture of cultures* during the later Second Intermediate Period culminated in the *wholesale adoption of Egyptian burial and religious practices* in the early New Kingdom. *The adoption was too rapid and widespread to have been produced by force alone,* and the prosperity and familiarity with Egypt that characterized the preceding period in Nubia shows that *it was not produced by mere acculturation* [emphasis added]. (84)

There is an "animal-headed human figure" made of fired clay (now housed at the University of California, Museum of Cultural History [see Illustration]) which had been determined to be from the period between 1900 and 1550 B.C.E. (Wenig 1978, 123). Based on the layer of stratum in which it was found, it was a product of the so-called C-group culture. It was "a cult object or...a votive offering" (123). Steffen Wenig writes that "the figure clearly has a sheep's head....The only other animal-headed human figures from the Nile Valley...apart for the animal-headed representation of the gods of Egypt and Kush, belong to the Predynastic Period" (123). The figure represents a female, probably a goddess, who is pregnant, which is a rarely depicted image in the Nile Valley (123). Of particular interest is the following comment by Wenig:

> ...the ram sacred to Amun from before the early New Kingdom originally came from Nubia...and may have been worshipped by both the C-group people and those of the Kerma culture [emphasis added]. (123)

The ram's head in question (now part of the collection of the Boston Museum of Fine Arts) is determined to be from the period between 1750 and 1550 B.C.E. It is made of quartz and is approximately half life-size and was originally glazed (145). This is an example of the similarities of Kushite and Kemite culture, for:

> We may assume that sheep already had some religious significance in Nubia, since statuettes of these animals, to which a cultic or ritual function must be attributed, were made so soon after their introduction [emphasis added]. (145)

Another Egyptologist supports the view that the sacredness of the ram was due to an impetus from the south:

> Wildung[4] (1973) has shown that the ram which from before the beginning of the New Kingdom was sacred to Amun reached Egypt from Nubia. Whether the ram was already connected, in the Kerma culture, with a native deity corresponding to the

> Egyptian god cannot be determined. *It is important, however, that Egypt adopted impulses from the south, as the ram of Amun demonstrates* [emphasis added]. (146)

Other evidence, published in 1923, suggests rams were sacred in Nubian culture. It comes from Kerma, which is located in Upper Nubia. It was a culture that "might correspond both to Yam and to the conjectural Upper Nubian kingdom with which XII Dynasty [of] Egypt traded" (Adams 1977, 195). Reisner excavated the eastern cemetery at Kerma. It is close to Napata because he relates that from there one could "take a short cut across the desert to (Napata)...in two days" (Reisner I-III 1923, 535). He dates the period from "about 1935 B.C. until 1580 B.C., or for more than three hundred and fifty years (121)." Among the detailed, 528-page report, he provides information concerning certain graves that indicated that rams had considerable sacred value to the people of Kerma. The items found at one of the tumuli (identified as K IV) included:

> Grave K 426—Ram found under bed (216)

> Grave K 441—"Bed-burial under hide, with at least four sacrificial bodies and a ram" (231)

> Grave K 446—"Ram lay incomplete on debris and the vessels in the grave were on debris" (236)

Reisner declares that the items found here are similar to those in another grave site excavated:

> The chief body was laid on a bed on the southern side of an open pot; the weapons, ornaments, utensils (headrest, fan, sandals, toilet implements, stone vessels), were placed on the bed....a certain number of members of the family of the chief, *together*

with one or more rams, were placed in the grave; and the whole was filled with earth. [emphasis added] (254)

In more recent excavations at Kerma, conducted by Charles Bonnet from 1975 to 1991, more evidence was found linking Nubia to Amun. In the burial sites, it appears that "the deposition of sheep became systematic. Some wore on their heads a disc of ostrich feathers...."[5] (Bonnet 1992, 622). That Bonnet is inclined to make a link to Amun is implied in his statement that "[i]nterpretation of the rock-engravings of the Sahara, which represent sheep with frontal discs and neck pendants, rather tends towards magic or religious significance. One is unavoidably led to think of ram-headed Amon who appeared in Egypt several centuries later—but it would be a delicate matter to trace a direct link" (622).

There is no hard evidence that would support an unequivocal statement that the worship of Amun began in Nubia. We can state that rams as spiritualized animals or totems were a part of the culture of Nubia before the rise of Amun during the 18th Dynasty. There was a synthesis of tradition between Kemet and Kush that allowed the swift and thorough acceptance of Amun to become intertwined into the whole organism of both cultures.

There are cultural similarities in Africa. Ancient Egypt and Kush were great cultures, and it is reasonable to assume that interchanges of ideas and goods occurred in both directions. The reason that evidence to support this theory has not been accumulated in one place before is probably because other scholars were more interested in asserting the superiority of the so-called Near East.

NOTES

1. This definition was suggested by Dr. Wade Nobles.

2. An anthropological term meaning, "either of two primary subdivisions in some tribes" (*Webster's New World Dictionary of the American Language* 1968:947).

3. He is considered to be the ancestor of the Yoruba.

4. This refers to a paper presented to the International Congress of Orientalists, Paris, July 1973 by D. Wildung, "Der widdergestaltige Amun-Ikonographie einer Gotterbildes." I have been unsuccessful in obtaining a copy of the original.

5. We do not know what the feather represented to the people of Kerma. However, in Kemet, the feather "appears as the sign of the goddess of truth and order, Maát...Thus the feather is often shown as a symbol of truth weighed against the heart...of the deceased in funerary judgement scenes" (Wilkinson 1992:103). Reisner (1923) also reported that ostrich feathers and fans were found in the grave which he excavated at Kerma. It does suggest that the feathers also had some spiritual value.

CHAPTER EIGHT

NOT THE END: SUMMARY, RECOMMENDATIONS, AND CONCLUSION

> ....Until the basic human rights
> Are equally guaranteed to all
> without regard to race
> that until that day, the dream of
> lasting peace, world citizenship and
> the rule of international morality
> will remain in but a fleeting illusion
> to be pursued, but never attained....
> --Bob Marley,
> *Rastaman Vibration*

Diop left a legacy. He laid the foundation upon which to build a new Afrocentric methodology. The present author has sought to contribute to a method of perceiving commonalities in Africa. The concepts--divine kingship, matriarchy, totemism, and cosmogony--are useful ones with which to analyze African cultures. There is more work to be done. However, if African people throughout the diaspora are ever to function as a political entity, they must first be aware of cultural commonalities.

Diop postulated that circumcision, social organization, and language are also useful concepts to determine a Negro origin of Kemet. I have dealt with social organization when examining matriarchy, but more needs to be done. Unfortunately, little is known about the common people of Kush. However, there is still a wealth of information in museum basements. Perhaps more will be revealed in the future. There is some evidence of circumcision, but more research should be undertaken on this topic. Theophile Obenga has accomplished a tremendous feat in tracing African languages from Kemet to other parts of Africa. When the language of Meroe is deciphered, a wealth of information will emerge.

This study can be valuable, however, in the context of the present. The idea of divine kingship and its prevalence throughout Africa may assist us in modern times to understand the relationship between African people throughout the diaspora and the leaders of the African diaspora. There is a long tradition in African culture of leaders with absolute power. The difference, however, was that ancient rulers were guided by *Maát*. They lived in Maát and by Maát and ruled because of Maát. They were expected to use power justly, because they had to answer for their deeds in order to achieve eternal life. African people have to reexamine leadership and establish a firm basis of accountability.

Our examination of issues surrounding matriarchy revealed that women had a primary position in Kushite and Kemetic culture. They ruled empires, fought battles, and were highly revered. In Greece, women were not allowed outside the house without their husbands. Not so in Africa. Kush prospered because of the abilities of males *and* females in leadership positions. Today African people throughout the world are under siege. Throughout the world, many African people are living in wretched poverty. African people need a multitude of resources to respond to inequalities. African men and women are affected by racism and social injustice. Women need to be accepted for all of their abilities.

The primacy of spirituality in African cultures can be demonstrated through totemism and cosmogony. Africans have always lived on material and spiritual levels simultaneously. Spirituality is so much a part of the tapestry of African culture that it cannot be separated without unraveling the whole cloth. In Africa, everything was spiritual. Animals and natural objects were all seen as spiritualized objects that were part of the divine order. Spirituality was so important, in the past, that African people need to learn how to use it for the betterment of Africans throughout the diaspora, in the present.

******

We Africans will fight, if necessary
And we know we will win
As we are confident in the victory of
Good over evil, of Good over evil....
--Bob Marley,
Rastaman Vibration

The historiography of African people has been distorted, demeaned, and diminished by people who do not represent the interests of African people. I have sought to demonstrate that the achievement of Kush has been inaccurately credited to external influences. Placing Kush within the framework of an Afrocentric paradigm reveals a more vigorous and vital culture; a culture from which other African cultures sought and received inspiration. The Afrocentric perspective can be used to shine new light on old data, so that a wealth of information illuminates the dark corners of the Eurocentric perspective. We must continue to burrow through the tunnels of hidden African history. May the ancestors be satisfied.

GLOSSARY

Africa-centered perspective: term developed by C.T. Keto, which posits Africa as a geographical and cultural starting point for the study of African people.

Africology: "the Afrocentric study of phenomena, events, ideas and personalities related to Africa" that uses the starting point of classical Africa as the beginning of knowledge (Asante 1990:14, 141).

African cultural holism: perspective that there are practices common to African cultures. In Chapter 7 of his *African Origin of Civilization* ([1955] 1974) Cheikh Anta Diop defined them as: totemism, circumcision, divine kingship, cosmogony, social organization, matriarchy, kinship of African languages with the language of Kemet.

African world-view: comprehensive ideas and values concerning order which allows one to perceive and understand the world.

Afrocentricity: social theory placing African ideals at the center of any analysis that involves culture and behavior.

Beheading of Africa: the practice of separating Egypt and Nubia from the rest of Africa.

Candaces: a series of queens of Meroe.

Cosmogony: a people's assumptions or beliefs about the origins of the universe.

Ethnic group: a social group which sets itself apart from other social groups on account of specific cultural traits, not only in a few details (such as food or clothing), but also in a complex of fundamental options (e.g., cosmogony, system of values, political organization) (Preiswerk and Perrot 1978:5).

Ethnocentricism: "the attitude of a group which consists of attributing to itself a central position compared to other groups, valuing positively its achievements and particular characteristics, adopting a projective type of behavior toward out-groups and interpreting the out-group through the in-group's mode of thinking" (Preiswerk and Perrot 1978:14).

Ethiopia: in ancient times, identified by Homer and Herodotus as including the Sudan, Egypt, Arabia, Palestine, Western Asia, and India (Jackson [1970] 1993:66)

Eurocentricism: a philosophy based in the values, world-view, and cultural roots of Europe.

Kemet: the name of Ancient Egypt, given by its ancient inhabitants, meaning "black."

Kemetologist: one who specializes in the study of ancient Egypt from an Afrocentric perspective.

Kush: the area covering the two successive ancient kingdoms of Napata and Meroe.

Maát: "Ra creates the universe through *Maát*, a term with multiple meanings, i.e., righteousness, truth, justice, order, harmony, rightness, evenness, levelness, etc....it is a divine concept, power and practice. ...[which] was established as the fundamental concept..." (Karenga [1984] 1989:4); "The Kemetic qualities of order, justice, righteousness, balance" (Asante 1990:83).

Meroe: capital city of the kingdom of Kush. Incorrectly called an island, it is the area of the Butanna Steepe, which lies between the Nile and the Atbara River.

Napata: a site located near the sacred mountain of Jebel Barkal; the first site of the kingdom of Kush.

Negro: first used as an adjective by the Portuguese involved in the *maafa* of the enslavement of Africans. "It was in the development of this infamous, iniquitous, and inhuman slave traffic that the term 'negro' was foisted as a noun, as a designation, as a name, upon those who were unfortunate enough to be caught in the clutches of the slave traders" (Moore [1960] 1990:36-7).

Nubia: not a modern political entity. The area known by this term (coined during the Christian era), lies today partly in Egypt and partly in the Republic of Sudan. Lower Nubia includes the area between the first [sixth] and second [fifth] cataracts. The valley south of the second [fifth] cataract to the fifth [second] cataract, the end of the Abu Hamed Reach, is called Upper Nubia.

Phenotype: a type distinguished by visible characteristics rather than by hereditary or genetic traits (Webster).

Principle of Consubstantiality: developed by Wade Nobles; states that the "elements of the universe are of one substance. With the essence being of the same stuff, the ancient African law of transformation and the later practice of substitution....makes sense. One can only have a conception of growth which results from the Jackal function if the essence of things is the same....The essence or essentialness of all things is spirit" (Nobles 1986:106).

Race: "the progeny of a fairly stable gene pool which produces people with similar physical characteristics" (Asante 1990:17).

Racism: "attributing to biological heredity the cultural peculiarities of a group which has highly distinctive physical features....the subjectivity of the racist [is] accepted as a fundamental element....identification by color is today a fact which affects relations between different races" (Preiswerk and Perrot 1978:16-17).

Somatic: of the body, physical (Webster).

Tribe: "a vague [category] in Africa....does not really imply any political unity or even, in many cases, the possession of a common language; for when we refer to the Ibo tribe, we are embracing under this head a congeries of peoples so diverse in language that two towns within a few miles of each other could hardly communicate with one another in pre-European days; as the Ibo territory covers thousands of square miles and the people number some four millions, it is clear that the term tribe is, strictly speaking, a misnomer..." (Thomas 1921:7).

Valorization: when people attribute positive or negative affect to a known object. "The value is projected on to the object, attributed to the object by man without necessarily being aware of it. He may truly believe that the value 'resides' in the object....Valorization is therefore an affective liaison, conscious or not, between the subject and the object, which can never be excluded from cognitive behavior. It is illusional to think that the methodological rigor imposed by scientific procedure could eliminate completely from the cognitive process that which is intrinsic to thought" (Preiswerk and Perrot 1978:33).

SELECTED BIBLIOGRAPHY

Adams, S. with J. Vercoutter. "The Importance of Nubia: A Link between Central Africa and the Mediterranean." In *The General History of Africa. Vol. II: Ancient Civilizations of Africa*, ed. G. Mohkhtar. Berkeley, Calif.: University of California Press, 1981.

Adams, William Y. *Nubia: Corridor to Africa.* Princeton, N.J.: Princeton University Press, 1977.

_____. "Doubts About the Lost Pharaohs." *Journal of Near Eastern Studies* 44, 1 (1985):185-192.

_____. "Post-Pharaonic Nubia In the Light of Archaeology." *Journal of Egyptian Archaeology* 50 (1950):102-120.

Amadiume, Ifi. *Afrikan Matriarchal Foundations: The Igbo Case.* London: Karnak House, 1987 [a].

_____. *Male Daughters, Female Husbands: Gender and Sex in An African Society.* London: Zed Books Ltd., 1987 [b].

Ani, Marimba. *Yurugu: An Africa-Centered Critique of European Cultural Thought and Behavior.* Trenton, N.J.: Africa World Press, 1994.

Asante, Molefi K. *Afrocentricity.* Trenton, N.J.: Africa World Press, 1988.

_____. *Kemet, Afrocentricity and Knowledge.* Trenton, N.J.: Africa World Press, 1990.

Batrawi, A. "The Racial History of Egypt and Nubia: Part I." *Journal of Royal Anthropological Institute of Great Britain and Ireland*, 75 (1945):81-101.

_____. "The Racial History of Egypt and Nubia: Part II." *Journal of Royal Anthropological Institute of Great Britain and Ireland*, 76 (1946):131-146.

Ben-Jochannan, Yosef. *Africa: Mother of Civilization*. Baltimore: Black Classics Press, 1971.

_____. *Black Man of the Nile and His Family*. New York: Alkebu-Lan Books, 1981.

Bernal, Martin. *Black Athena: The Afroasiatic Roots of Classical Civilization*. Vol. I. *The Fabrication of Ancient Greece, 1785-1985*. New Brunswick, N.J.: Rutgers University Press, 1987.

Blackman, Aylward. "The Pharaoh's Placenta and the Moon-God Khons." *Journal of Egyptian Archaeology* 3 (1916):235-249.

Bonnet, Charles. "Excavations at Nubian Kerma 1975-91." *Antiquity* 66, 252 (September 1992):611-25.

Breasted, James H. *Ancient Records of Egypt: From the Earliest Times to The Persian Conquest*. Vols. I & IV. New York: Charles Scribner & Sons, 1906 & 1912.

Browder, Anthony T. *Exploding The Myths: Nile Valley Contributions to Civilization*, Vol. I. Washington, D.C.: The Institute of Karmic Guidance, 1992.

Budge, E. A. W. *The Gods of the Egyptians*, Vol II. London: Methuen & Co. 1904.

_____. *An Egyptian Hieroglyphic Dictionary*, Vols. I & II. New York: Dover Publications, [1920] 1978.

_____. *The Egyptian Book of the Dead*. New York: Dover Publications, [1895] 1967.

Buttles, Janet. *The Queens of Egypt.* London: Archibald Constable & Co., 1908.

Carruthers, Jacob H. *Essays in Ancient Egyptians Studies.* Los Angeles: University of Sankore Press, 1984.

Chadwick, Douglass H. "Ndoki: Last Place on Earth: The Pygmy Way." *National Geographic Magazine* (July 1995):2-40.

Clark, John H., ed. *Black Titan: W.E.B. DuBois: An Anthology.* Boston: Beacon Press, 1970.

Collins, Robert O. *Problems in African History.* Englewood Cliffs, N.J.: Prentice Hall, Inc., 1943.

Connah, Graham. *African Civilizations: Precolonial Cities and States in Tropical Africa: An Archeological Perspective.* New York: Cambridge University Press, 1987.

Curtin, Philip. *African History.* London: Longman, 1990.

Davidson, Basil. *A History of West Africa to the Nineteenth Century.* New York: Anchor Books, 1966.

_____. *The Lost Cities of Africa.* Boston: Little, Brown & Co., 1966.

_____. *East and Central Africa to the Late Nineteenth Century.* Garden City, N.Y.: Doubleday & Co., 1966.

_____. *A History of East Africa to the Nineteenth Century.* Garden City, N.Y.: Doubleday & Co. 1959.

DeGraft-Johnson, John C. *African Glory.* New York: Walker & Co., 1966.

Depuydt, Leo. "The Date of Piye's Egyptian Campaign and the Chronology of the Twenty-fifth Dynasty." *Journal of Egyptian Archaeology* 79 (1993):269-274.

Diop, Cheikh Anta. *The African Origin of Civilization: Myth or Reality.* Westport, CT.: Lawrence Hill & Co., [1955] 1974.

_____. "Origin of the Ancient Egyptians." In *The General History of Africa: Ancient Civilizations of Africa* Vol. II, ed. G. Mohktar. Berkeley, CA: University of California Press, 1981.

_____. Report of the Symposium on "The Peopling of Ancient Egypt and the Deciphering of the Meroitic Script." In *The General History of African: Ancient Civilizations of Africa*, II. ed. G. Mohktar. Berkeley, CA: University of California Press, 1981.

_____. *Civilization or Barbarism: An Anthropology.* Brooklyn, NY: Lawrence Hill Books, [1981] 1991.

_____. *The Cultural Unity of Black Africa.* Chicago: Third World Press, 1978.

Diodorus Siculus. *Diodorus Of Sicily*, Vols. I & II. Cambridge, MA: Harvard University Press, [1933] 1989.

Dixon, D.M. "The Origin of the Kingdom of Kush." *Journal of Egyptian Archaeology* 50 (1964):121-132.

Drake, St. Clair. *Black Folk Here and There.* Los Angeles: Center for Afro-American Studies, 1987.

DuBois, W.E.B. *Black Folk Then and Now.* New York: Henry Holt & Co., 1939.

_____. *The World and Africa.* New York: Viking Press, [1946] 1968.

Dunham, Dows. "Outline of the Ancient History of the Sudan." *Sudan Notes And Records* 28 (1947):1-10.

_____. *The Royal Cemeteries of Kush.* London: Cambridge University Press, 1965.

Dunham, Dows and M.F. Macadam. "Names and Relationships of the Royal Family of Napata." *Journal of Egyptian Archaeology* 35 (1949):139-149.

Selected Bibliography

Dolinska, Monika. "Red and Blue Figures of Amun." *Varia Aegyptiaca* 6, 1-2 (April-August, 1990):3-7.

Emery, Walter. *Egypt in Nubia*. London: Hutchinson & Co., 1965.

Erman, Adolf. *Life in Ancient Egypt*. London: MacMillian and Co., 1894.

Fage, J. D. *A History of West Africa*. London: Cambridge University Press, 1960.

Ferlini, Guiseppe. Cenno sugli scavi operati nella Nubia e Catalogo degli oggetti rivitrovate. Bologna, 1837.

_____. "Relation historique des foilles operees dans le Nubie." Rome, 1838.

Foster, John. *Love Songs of the New Kingdom*. New York: Charles Scribner's Sons, 1973.

Frankfort, Henri. *Kingship and the Gods*. Chicago: University of Chicago Press, 1948.

_____. "Modern Survivors From Punt." In *Studies Presented to F. LL. Griffith*. London: Oxford University Press, 1932.

Frazer, James George. *Adonis Attis Osiris: Studies in the History of Oriental Religion*. New York: University Books, 1961.

_____. *Taboo and the Perils of the Soul*. London: MacMillian and Co., 1919.

_____. *The Golden Bough: The Dying God*. London: MacMillian and Co., 1919.

_____. *Totemism and Exogamy*. London: MacMillian and Co., 1935.

_____. *Totemism*. Edinburgh: Adam & Charles Black, 1887.

Gardiner, Alan H. "Piankhi's Instructions To His Army." *Journal Of Egyptian Archaeology*. 21 (1935):219-223.

_____. *Egyptian Grammar*. London: Griffith Institute, [1927] 1994.

_____. *Egypt of the Pharaohs: An Introduction*. New York: Holt, Rinehart and Winston, 1961.

Griffith, F. LL. *Meroitic Inscriptions*. London: The University Press, 1911.

_____. "Meroitic Studies VI." *Journal of Egyptian Archeology* 15 (1929):69-74.

_____. *Meroitic Inscriptions. Part I. Soba To Dangel*. London: Egypt Exploration Fund, 1911.

_____. "Meroitic Studies." *Journal of Egyptian Archaeology* 3 (1916):22-30, 111-124.

_____. "Meroitic Studies IV.: The Great Stela of Prince Akinzaz." *Journal of Egyptian Archaeology* 4 (1917):159-173.

Hakem, A. A. "The Civilization of Napata and Meroe." In *The General History of Africa*, II. Berkeley, CA.: University of California Press, 1981:172-202.

Hansberry, William. *Sources for the Study of Ethiopian History*. Washington, DC: Howard University Press, 1931.

_____. *Pillars in Ethiopian History*. Washington: Howard University Press, 1974.

Harris, Joseph. *African and Their History*. New York: New American Library, 1972.

_____, ed. *The Legacy of Egypt*. London: Oxford University Press, 1971.

Haynes, Joyce. *Nubia: Ancient Kingdoms of Africa*. Boston: Museum of Fine Arts, 1994.

Hegel, Georg W. *The Philosophy of History*. New York: The Colonial Press, 1899.

Hintze, Fritz. "The Kingdom of Kush: The Meroitic Period." *Africa in Antiquity: The Arts of Ancient Nubia and the Sudan*. Brooklyn, NY: The Brooklyn Museum, 1978.

Hoffman, Michael. *Egypt Before the Pharaohs*. New York: Dorset Press, 1979.

Houston, Drusilla D. *The Wonderful Ethiopians and the Ancient Cushite Empire*. Baltimore, MD: Black Classic Press, 1926.

Huntingford, G.W.B. "Egypt in Africa." *Ancient Egypt*. IV. London: MacMillan & Co., 1925:98-99.

_____. "Egypt and the Masai." *Ancient Egypt*. I. London: MacMillian & Co., 1926:10-11.

Jackson, J. W. "The Antiquity of Civilization." *Journal of Anthropology*. London: Longman, Green & Co., 1870, 1871, 170-180.

Jackson, John. *Introduction to African Civilization*. New York: Citadel Press, 1970.

Jahn, Janheinz. *Muntu: African Culture and the Western World*. New York: Grove Weidenfeld, [1961] 1989.

James, George. *Stolen Legacy: The Greeks Were Not the Authors of Greek Philosophy, But the People of North Africa, Commonly Called the Egyptians*. San Francisco: Julian Richardson Associates [original ed.], 1954.

Jeffreys, M.D. W. "The Diffusion of Cowries and Egyptian Culture in Africa." *American Anthropologist*, 50, Menasha, WI: The American Anthropological Association, 1948:45-53.

Jordan, Winthrop. *White Over Black: American Attitudes Toward the Negro, 1550-1812*. Kingsport, TN: The University of North Carolina Press, 1968.

Junker, Hermann. "The First Appearance of the Negroes in History." *Journal of Egyptian Archeology*. London: The Egyptian Exploration Society, 1921:121-132.

Karenga, Maulana. *Introduction to Black Studies*. Los Angeles: The University of Sankore Press, 1993.

_____. *Selections From the Husia: Sacred Wisdom of Ancient Egypt*. Los Angeles: University of Sankore Press, 1984.

Karenga, Maulana and Jacob H. Carruthers. *Kemet and the African Worldview: Research and Restoration*. Los Angeles: The University of Sankore Press, 1986.

Keto, C.T. *The Africa-Centered Perspective of History*. Blackwood NJ: K.A. Publications, 1989.

Ki-Zerbo, J., ed. *General History of Africa, I: Methodology and African Prehistory*. Berkeley, CA: University of California Press, 1990.

Lefkowitz, Mary "Influential Women." *Images of Women In Antiquity*. Ed. Averil Cameron and Amelie Kuhrt. Detroit, MI: Wayne State University Press, 1983.

Lesko, Barbara. "Researching The Role of Women In Ancient Egypt." *KMT: A Modern Journal of Ancient Egypt* 5, 4 (Winter 1994-1995):14-23.

Levi-Strauss, Claude. *Totemism*. London: Penguin Books, [1962] 1973.

_____. *The Elementary Structures of Kinship*. Boston: Beacon Press, 1969.

Litchtheim, Miriam. *Ancient Egyptian Literature: A Book of Readings*, I, II, III. Los Angeles: University of California, 1975, 1976, 1980.

Macadam, M.F. *The Temples of Kawa: I. The Inscriptions*. London: The Griffith Institute, 1949.

_____."Queen Nawidemak." *Bulletin of the Allen Memorial Art Museum, Oberlin College* 23, 2 (1966):42-71.

Manniche, Lisa. "Divine Reflections of Female Behavior." *KMT: A Modern Journal of Ancient Egypt* 5, 4 (Winter 1994-1995):53-59.

Mbiti, John S. *African Religions and Philosophy*. New York: Anchor Books, 1970.

McFeely, William. *Frederick Douglass*. New York: W. W. Norton & Co., 1991.

Meyerowitz, Eva. "Concepts of the Soul Among the Akan of the Gold Coast." *Africa*, 21 London: Oxford University Press, 1951:24-31.

Millet, N. B. and A. Kelley, eds. *Meroitic Studies: Proceedings of the Third International Meroitic Conference*. Berlin: Akademie-Verlag, 1982.

Moore, Richard. *The Name "Negro" Its Origin And Evil Use*. Baltimore, MD: Black Classic Press, [1960] 1992.

Moret, A. and G. Davy. *From Tribe To Empire*. New York: Alfred A. Knopf, 1926.

Mukherjee, Rao. *The Ancient Inhabitants of Jebel Moya (Sudan)*. London: Cambridge University Press, 1955.

Murdock, George P. *Social Structure*. New York: The Free Press, 1949.

_____. *Africa: Its People and their Culture History*. New York: McGraw Hill, 1959.

Murray, M.A. "An Early Sed-Festival." *Ancient Egypt*. Part III (September, 1932):70-72.

"Nubian Treasures Reflect Black Influence on Egypt." *New York Times,* February 11, 1992:C-10.

"Of Pygmies and Princes." *Newsweek*, October, 1992:60.

Nobles, Wade. "Ancient Egyptian Thought and the Renaissance of African (Black) Psychology." In *Kemet and the African Worldview*, ed. Maulana Karenga with Jacob Carruthers. Los Angeles: University of Sankore Press, 1985.

_____. *African Psychology*. Oakland, CA: The Black Family Institute, 1987.

Obenga, Theophile. "African Philosophy of the Pharaonic Period." In *Egypt Revisited*, ed. Ivan Van Sertima. New Brunswick, NJ: Transaction Publishers, 1989.

Oliver, Roland with G. Matthews. *History of East Africa, I*. London: Clarendon Press, 1963.

Olson, Stacie, and J. Wegner. *Ancient Nubia: Egypt's Rival in Africa*. Philadelphia, PA: University Museum of Archeology and Anthropology, University of Pennsylvania, 1992.

Ortega y Gasset, Jose. *An Interpretation of Universal History*. New York: W.W. Norton & Co., 1973.

Petrie, Flinders. "Egypt in Africa, I." *Ancient Egypt*. Part III. London: MacMillian and Co., 1914:115-127.

Pimienta-Bey, Jose. "Moorish Spain: Academic Source and Foundation for the Rise and Success of Western European Universities in the Middle Ages." In *Golden Age Of The Moor*, ed. Ivan Van Sertima. New Brunswick, NJ: Transaction Press, 1993.

Pliny. *Natural History*. II. Cambridge, Mass.: Harvard University Press, [1942] 1989.

Preiswerk, Roy with Dominique Perrot. *Ethnocentrism and History: Africa, Asia and Indian America in Western Textbooks*. New York: Nok Publishers International, 1978.

Priese, Karl-Heinz. *The Gold Of Meroe*. New York: The Metropolitan Museum of Art, 1993.

_____. "The Kingdom of Kush: The Napatan Period." In *Africa in Antiquity: The Arts of Ancient Nubia and the Sudan*. Brooklyn, NY: The Brooklyn Museum, 1978.

Reeder, Greg. "Ritual Death and Rebirth: Running the Heb Sed." *KMT: A Modern Journal of Ancient Egypt* 4, 4 (Winter 1993-94):60-71.

Reisner, G.A. "The Pyramids of Meroe and the Candaces of Ethiopia." *Sudan Notes and Records* 4 (1922):173-196.

_____. *Ancient Egypt and Black Africa*. London: Karnak House, 1992.

_____. *Excavations At Kerma*. Parts IV.-V. Cambridge, MA: Peabody Museum of Harvard University, 1923 [a].

_____. "Outline of the Ancient History of the Sudan" Parts I, II, III. *Sudan Notes and Records*. 1 (1918):3-67.

_____. "The Meroitic Kingdom Of Ethiopia: A Chronological Outline." *Journal of Egyptian Archeology*, 9 (1923[b]):34-76.

Renfrew, Colin and Paul Bahn. *Archeology: Theories, Methods, and Practice*. London: Thames & Hudson LTD, 1991.

Robins, Gay. *Women In Ancient Egypt*. Cambridge, MA: Harvard University Press, 1993.

_____. "The God's Wife of Amun in the 18th Dynasty in Egypt." In *Images of Women In Antiquity,* eds. Averil Cameron and Amelie Kuhrt. Detroit, MI: Wayne State University Press, 1983.

Said, Edward W. *Orientalism*. New York: Vantage Books Edition, 1979.

Save-Soderbergh, T. "A Buhen Stela From the Second Intermediate Period (Khartoum 18)." *Journal of Egyptian Archaeology* 35 (1949):50-58.

_____, ed. *Temples and Tombs of Ancient Nubia*. New York: Thames and Hudson Inc., 1987.

Seligman, C. G. "Egyptian Influence in Negro Africa." In *Studies Presented To F. LL. Griffith*. London: Oxford University Press, 1932.

_____. *Egypt and Negro Africa: A Study in Divine Kingship*. London: George Rutledge & Sons, Ltd., 1934.

_____. *Races of Africa*. London: Oxford University Press, [1930] 1957.

Shinnie, Margaret. *Ancient African Kingdoms*. New York: Signet Classics, 1965.

Shinnie, Paul. "Trade Routes of the Ancient Sudan." In *Egypt and Africa: Nubia From Prehistory to Islam*, ed. W.V. Davies. London: British Museum Press, 1991.

_____. *Meroe: A Civilization of the Sudan*. New York: Frederick A. Preager, 1967.

Shinnie, Paul and Francoise Kense. "Meroitic Iron Working." In *Meroitic Studies: Proceedings of the Third International Meroitic Conference*, eds. Millet, N.B. & Kelley, Allyn. Berlin: Akademie-Verlag, 1982.

Schneider & Gough (eds.). *Matrilineal Kinship*. Berkeley, CA: University of California Press, 1961.

Smith, G. Elliot. *The Ancient Egyptians and Their Influence Upon the Civilization of Europe*. London: Harper and Brothers, 1911.

Snowden, Frank. *Blacks in Antiquity: Ethiopians in the Greco-Roman Experience*. Cambridge, MA: Harvard Press, 1970.

"Special Report: Egypt and Nubia." *KMT: A Modern Journal of Ancient Egypt* 3, 3 (Fall 1992):27-39.

Strabo. *The Geography of Strabo*. Vols. I, VII, & VIII. Cambridge, MA: Harvard University Press, [1932] 1982.

Taylor, John H. *Egypt and Nubia*. Cambridge, MA: Harvard University Press, 1991.

Thomas, N.W. "Burial Rites of West Africa." *Ancient Egypt*. Part I. London: MacMillian and Co., 1921:7-13.

Thompson, Robert. *African Art in Motion*. Los Angeles: University of California Press, 1974.

Thomas, N.W. "Dualism In African Religions." *Ancient Egypt*, Part IV. London: 1922, 198-109.

Toynbee, Arnold. *A Study of History*. London: Oxford University Press, 1934.

Trigger, Bruce. *Nubia Under the Pharaohs*. Boulder, CO: Westview Press, 1976.

_____. "Nubian, Negro, Black, Nilotic?" In *Africa in Antiquity: The Arts Of Ancient Nubia and the Sudan*. Brooklyn, NY: Brooklyn Museum, I, 1978.

_____. "Monumental Architecture: A Thermodynamic Explanation of Symbolic Behavior." *World Archaeology* 22 (1991).

Uphill, Eric. "The Egyptian Sed-Festival Rites." *Journal of Near Eastern Studies* 24 (January-October, 1965):365-383.

Van Sertima, Ivan. *They Came Before Columbus, The African Presence in America*. New York: Random House, 1976.

_____. *Golden Age of the Moors*. New York: Random House, 1992.

Vansina, Jan. *Oral Tradition as Tradition*. Madison, WI: The University of Wisconsin Press, 1985.

Vinogradov, A.K. "*Diodorus on the Election of Kings of Meroe*." In *Meroitica: Studia Meroitica 1984*. Berlin: Akademie-Verlag, 1989.

Vycichl, Werner. "The Present State of Meroitic Studies." *Kush* 6 (1958):74-81.

Wainwright, G. A. "Some Aspects of Amun." *Journal of Egyptian Archaeology* 20 (1932):140-172.

_____. "Letopolis." *Journal of Egyptian Archeology* 28, 132 (159-172).

Waterson, Barbara. *Women in Ancient Egypt*. New York: St. Martin's Press, 1991.

Weigall, Arthur. *Personalities of Antiquity*. New York: H.W. Wilson Co., 1932.

Welsh-Asante, Kariamu. "Commonalities in African Dance: An Aesthetic Foundation." In *African Culture: The Rhythms of Unity*, eds. Molefi Asante and Kariamu Welsh-Asante. Trenton, NJ: Africa World Press, [1985] 1990.

Wenig, Steffen. *Africa in Antiquity: Arts of Ancient Nubia and Sudan*. Vols. I & II. Brooklyn, NY: The Brooklyn Museum, 1978.

White, J. E. Manchip. *Ancient Egypt: Its Culture and History*. New York: Dover Publications, Inc., 1970.

Williams, Bruce. "The Lost Pharaohs of Nubia." *Archeology*. 33, 5 (1980):12-21.

_____. "The Lost Pharaohs of Nubia." In *Egypt Revisited*. [Reprint] *Journal of African Civilization*. Vol.4, No.2. New Brunswick, NJ: Rutgers University, 1982.

_____. "A Prospectus for Exploring the Historical Essence of Ancient Nubia." In *Egypt and Africa: Nubia From Prehistory to Islam*, ed. W. V. Davies. London: British Museum Press, 1991.

_____. "Forebears of Menes in Nubia: Myth or Reality?" *Journal of Near Eastern Studies* 46, 1 (1987):15-26.

Williams, Bruce and Thomas J. Logan. "The Metropolitan Museum Knife Handle and Aspects of Pharaonic Imagery Before Narmer." *Journal Of Near Eastern Studies*, 46 4 (1987):245-287.

Williams, Chancellor. *The Destruction of Black Civilization*. Chicago: Third World Press, 1974.

Williams, Larry. *The Struggle to Bring True African History into Being*. Los Angeles: The Association For the Study of Classical African Civilizations, 1992.

Wilkinson, Richard. *Reading Egyptian Art: A Hieroglyphic Guide to Ancient Egyptian Painting and Sculpture*. London: Thames & Hudson Ltd., 1994.

Winlock, H.E. "Notes on Jewels from Luhun." *Ancient Egypt*. Part III (1920):74-87.

INDEX

Abar, Queen, 120, 136
Adams, S., 23, 27; William, 21, 22, 24, 25, 29, 46, 48, 49, 94-96, 101, 141, 142, 146, 179
Africology, 46, 86, 191
Afrocentricity, 7, 30, 53, 63, 64, 191
Amadiume, Ifi, 129, 134
Amanirenas I, God's Wife of Amun, 146, 150; Amanirenas, Kandake, 146, 150
Amanishakheto, Kandake, 146-148, 150
Amenirdis, 139
Amun, (Amon) (Amen), 19, 81, 104, 115-117, 119-121, 135, 137, 139-140, 144, 176-179, 181-183
Ani, Marimba, 41, 48
Anlamani, King, 136, 140
Asante, culture, 134
Asante, Molefi, vii, 35, 44, 53, 63-65, 67, 86, 88, 102; Kariamu Welsh, 66
Auset, goddess, 2, 16, 104

Bachofen, J.J., 126, 127
Beer, 71, 117
Beheading, Africa, 21, 37, 45, 191
Ben-Jochannan, Yosef, 57

Blood, 1, 25, 37, 114, 158, 160, 161, 174
Blue, 177-178
Blyden, Edward Wilmot, 55
Bread, 117
Browder, Tony, 22, 196
Butanna, Steepe, 192

Candace(s), Kandake, 128,140 143, 145, 146, 152, 191
Carruthers, Jacob, 20, 21
Cataract(s), 19, 21, 23, 24, 27, 28, 32, 37, 51, 192
Chaka Zulu, King, 108
Consubstantiality, Principle of, 161, 193
Cosmogony, 31, 107, 152, 155, 172, 176, 177, 184, 185, 191
Cowries, 79

Davidson, Basil, 84, 85
Diffusion(ist), 43, 73, 78, 81 83, 85
Diop, Cheikh Anta, v, 17, 30-32, 39, 40, 50, 53, 58-60, 64-66, 88, 89, 91, 95, 96, 102, 106, 125-129, 132, 152, 155, 156, 158, 170, 172, 176, 184, 185, 191
Douglass, Frederick, 55
Drake, St. Clair, 57, 58, 144
Dualism, 74

DuBois, W.E.B., 30, 52-54

Easton, Hosea, 55
Ergamenes, King, 112-114
Ethiopia(n), 17, 21, 23, 37, 54-56, 87, 111-113, 115, 128, 140, 142, 143, 145, 192
Ethnocentrism, 47, 48
Eurocentrism, 48, 86

Falcon, 59, 77, 92, 93, 151, 155, 163-166, 179
Feast of Opet, 117
Frazer, James, 106, 107, 108, 130, 133, 156-159, 161

God's Wife of Amun, 137-140
Goddesses, 2, 16, 86, 102, 104, 144, 178, 181; Auset, 2, 16, 104; Hathor, 16; Nabhet, 104
Gods, 57, 85, 92, 103-107, 109, 112, 115-117, 119, 151, 159, 163, 176-178, 181; Amun, (Amon) (Amen), 19, 81, 104, 115-117, 119-121, 135, 137, 139-140, 144, 176-179, 181-183; Ptah, 119; Re, 117-119, 121, 135, 137; Thoth, 118
Greek(s), 17, 19, 20, 50, 55, 83, 111-114, 121, 132, 133, 157, 158, 173
Griffith, F.LL., 18, 77, 141, 142, 148, 149

Hamite(s), 27, 29, 31, 32, 35 38, 72, 77, 108
Hansberry, William Leo, 54, 55
Hathor, goddess, 16

Hatshepsut, Queen, 16, 33, 75, 81, 86, 92, 104, 139, 163
Hegel, Georg Wilheim, 44-49
Hermopolis, 115, 117, 118
Houston, Asa G., 56
Houston, Drusilla, 56, 57

Ibo, 71, 74, 79, 80, 81, 193

Jahn, Janheinz, 173, 174
Jebel Barkal, 18, 19, 150, 192, 203
Jeffreys, M., 79-83
Junker, Hermann, 29-32

Ka, vi, 74, 75, 163, 172, 174
Kandake, Amanirenas, 146, 150; Amanishakheto, 146-148, 150; Candace(s), 128, 140 143, 145, 146, 152, 191
Kemet(ic),(ites), vi, vii, 1, 3, 4-7, 22-26, 28, 30, 31, 33, 34, 39, 41, 42-44, 52, 53, 55-60, 63, 64, 69-72, 74, 75, 80, 81, 83, 88, 91, 93, 98-101, 103, 107, 109, 112, 114, 115, 120-122, 125, 131, 136-139, 147, 151, 163, 165, 175, 176, 177, 178, 179, 180, 183, 185, 191, 192
Kerma, 27, 43, 44, 59, 180-183
Keto, C.T., vi, 21, 28, 65, 84, 191
Killing, Ritual, 71, 102, 106, 108, 109, 112-114, 156, 158
Kings, vi, 1, 2, 18, 22, 25 29, 33, 37, 40, 44, 52, 56, 57, 59, 75-77, 82, 86, 90, 93, 94, 101-104, 106, 108-122, 132, 135-140, 145, 149-151, 163-166, 174, 177, 178;

Anlamani, 136, 140; Chaka Zulu, 108; Ergamenes, 112-114; Piankhi, vi, 2, 51, 59, 114-120, 139, 140; Rameses III, 115; Taharqa, 2, 120, 121, 135- 137, 140; Tutankhamen, 33, 56; Valley of, 1, 33,
Kingship, Divine, 22, 59, 81, 88-91, 93, 98, 100-104, 108, 109, 111, 112, 114, 121, 163, 166, 178, 184, 185, 191
Kintu, 173, 175
K(C)ush(ites), 1, 16-19, 24, 27-29, 31, 33, 39, 41-44, 52, 56-58, 60, 63-68, 89, 111, 112, 114, 117, 118, 121, 125, 126, 134, 135, 137, 140-142, 144, 147, 152, 153, 171, 174-179, 181, 183, 185, 186, 192

Lesko, Barbara, 133
Levi-Strauss, Claude, 131, 166-170
Locke, Alain, 56

Maát, 67, 92, 102, 104-106, 109, 113, 115, 116, 118, 119, 121, 132, 163, 177, 178, 185, 192
Matriarchy, 31, 120, 125-130, 132-134, 141, 152, 184, 185, 191
Matrilineal, 104, 125, 126, 128, 133, 134, 141, 142, 152
Mbiti, John, 47, 65, 107, 118, 171
Memphis, 119

Meroe (Merowe), 2-5, 40, 43, 57, 107, 111-113, 140, 142, 143, 146-148, 185, 191, 192
Mesopotamia(ns), 103, 104, 116
Muntu, 173-175

Nabhet, goddess, 104
Namlot, 117, 118
Nawidemak, Queen, 150-152
Nefertari, Queen, 2, 138, 139
Negative Confessions, 105; Image, 35, 45; Valorize(ation), 45, 48, 60, 127, 193; Values, 22
Negro, Name, 34-36
Nile, 1, 2, 21-23, 29, 57, 78, 85, 87, 88, 102, 149; River, 1, 5, 22, 23, 27, 57, 77, 107, 114, 115, 117, 127, 192; Valley, 21-24, 27, 31, 32, 34, 37, 39, 45, 47, 49, 52-60, 84, 90, 93, 95, 96, 100, 128, 137, 174, 178, 181
Nobles, Wade, vi, 54, 63, 67, 172, 193
Nommo, 174, 175
Northern Cradle, 127
Ntu, 16, 173
Nubia(n)(s), 1, 2, 3, 19-32, 35, 37-40, 42-44, 49, 51, 52, 55, 57-59, 70, 81, 87, 89-103, 110, 114, 120, 121, 141, 146, 180-183, 191, 192

Obenga, Theophile, 16, 17, 20, 53
Oriental Institute of Chicago, 89, 90
Orientation, 6-8, 64, 85, 133

Patriarchy, 126, 127

Petrie, Flinders, 69-72
Pharaoh, 4, 10, 29, 33, 57, 59, 91-94, 97-98, 103-105, 109, 110, 128, 155, 163-165
Phenotype, 31, 192
Piankhi, King, vi, 2, 51, 59, 114-120, 139, 140
Pliny, 143, 145
Ptah, god, 119
Punt(ites), 12, 27, 33, 72, 80, 81, 92
Pyramids, 1, 2, 42, 74, 103, 147, 174

Queen Mother, 134, 136
Queens, 1, 2, 20, 59, 75, 80, 85, 104, 125, 128, 12, 134, 136-146, 149-152, 166, 174, 191; Abar, 120, 136; Hapshepsut, 16, 33, 75, 81, 86, 92, 104, 139, 163; Nawidemak, 150-152; Nefertari, 2, 138, 139; Queen Mother, 134, 136
Qustal, 10, 90, 92, 95, 110

Rameses III, King, 115
Re, god, 117, 118, 119, 121, 135, 137
Regicide, 106, 107
Reisner, George, 4, 28, 43, 44, 46, 90, 97-100, 137, 141, 150, 182
Religions, African, 47, 73, 83, 106, 128, 156, 159, 160, 169, 180
Robins, Gay, 46, 138

Sahara, 21-24, 36-38, 40, 45, 60, 83, 84, 183; sub-Sahara, 21, 23, 36, 40, 45, 47, 60, 83

Script, Meroitic, 20, 140, 149
Sed festival, 81, 94, 109, 110
Seele, Keith, 90
Shabaka, 4
Shinnie, Margaret, 41, 42; Peter, 40, 41, 43, 45, 146
Snowden, Frank, 57, 111
Southern Cradle, 127
Strabo, 112, 113, 142, 143, 145
Sudan, 7, 8, 15, 19, 23, 32, 40-42, 59, 76, 77, 147, 192

Taharqa, King, 2, 120, 121, 135-137, 140
Ta-Seti, 10, 94
Tefnakhte, 115, 120
The Golden Bough, 106, 130
Thebes, 116, 120, 137, 139, 141, 176
Theory, Two Cradle Theory, 126, 127; Diffusionist, 81, 82
Thoth, god, 118
Totemism, 17, 155-171, 175, 184, 186, 191
Toynbee, Arnold, 49-51
Twinness, 73

Valorize(d)(ation), 19, 42, 45, 48, 60, 127, 193
Van Sertima, Ivan, 57, 59, 94

Walker, David, 55
Wawat, 10, 11, 13, 28
Wenig, Steffen 42, 144, 180
Williams, Bruce, 58, 59, 90-97, 110, 179; Chancellor, 57

Yam, 10-13, 101, 181